*Nog vele jaren*

# EACH YEAR OF LIFE

## ITS SYMBOLISM AND MEANING

# Nog vele jaren

## EACH YEAR OF LIFE

### ITS SYMBOLISM AND MEANING

by Hans Korteweg
illustrations by Erica Duvekot

■ HAZELDEN®

Hazelden
Center City, Minnesota  55012-0176
1-800-328-0094
1-612-257-1331 (FAX)
http://www.Hazelden.org

*Library of Congress Cataloging-in-Publication Data*
  Korteweg, Hans.
  [Nog vele jaren. English]
  Each year of life: its symbolism and meaning =
    Nog vele jaren/ by Hans Korteweg; illustra-
    tions by Erica Duvekot.
      p. cm.
    ISBN 1-56838-146-8
    1. Life. 2. Life cycle, Human. 3. Developmental
    psychology.
    BD431.K651413 1997
    158—dc21                              96-51697
                                              CIP

Translated by Mark DeSorgher
Text design by Nora Koch/Gravel Pit Publications

*Editor's note*
Hazelden offers a variety of information on chemi-
cal dependency and related areas. Our publications
do not necessarily represent Hazelden's programs,
nor do they officially speak for any Twelve Step
organization.

This book was set in Minion, Trajan, and Snell
Roundhand types and printed on 80 pound
Somerset Matte paper.

# CONTENTS

## PREFACE

This is a book about what is closer to us than anything else—our life, the life of one person from birth to 84. You might call it a book of life and a book for life. On each birthday, you can turn a page and read a new story—a prophecy of what lies ahead. Each year, you will find a new *quality* and a unique *possibility* as you grow toward happiness and fulfillment. You might imagine being given one very special present each year. Now you may unwrap the present and use its unique gift in your own life.

The miraculous thing here is that this gift is not one that can simply be taken for granted. It is a possibility, and it is we who decide what the gift will eventually look like by the way we unwrap it.

It is for this reason that I often introduce the gift to the reader in the beginning of my description of each year. I do not tell what kind of personal reactions or "possibilities of unwrapping" people often have until afterward. I start out by describing the numbers as entities.

When described this way, the numbers can be seen objectively, separate from the human personality. This means that the numbers can be applied to anything that has a certain life span, for example, the number of years people have had a personal or a working relationship, or the number of years a company has existed.

The individual years, when taken together, move like a wave through our lives. This wave encompasses three periods of twenty-eight years. Each period is divided again into four phases of seven years. These phases are very important, so this book makes it very clear which twenty-eight-year period we are in each year and which seven-year phase within that period. As we approach old age, the importance of individual years begin to decrease, while the importance of the phase increases. I have described the last fourteen years of the total eighty-four-year cycle as two seven-year phases, rather than as fourteen individual years. In the general commentary at the end of the book, I have explained the development and meaning of the phases in greater detail.

It was a great pleasure writing *Nog vele jaren*. In this one book, I could bring together all the knowledge and experience of a lifetime—my understanding of psychology, my love of myths and fairy tales, my fascination for numbers and cosmic patterns, and the total experience of all my years. Year by year, I have told the story of life in full. There is much to say about the philosophy behind this book, which I have tried to explain in the personal and general commentaries. It may be a good idea, if you want to better understand the ideas on which I have based my "book of life," to read these first, although I don't think it is essential. In general, the book speaks for itself.

What remains is to thank a number of people who have been involved in the creation of this book. I am immeasurably grateful to my teacher, Reinoud Fentener van Vlissingen. Without his totally unconditional support, this book could never have been written. Mrs. C. Korteweg, Piet Deunhouwer, and Rogier Fentener van Vlissingen have shown me the way at some crucial moments and/or have given me essential information.

Hanneke Korteweg-Frankhuisen and Jaap Voight have patiently helped me in finding the right form. Finally, Erica Duvekot has enriched the text with her heart-warming illustrations. My thanks go out to all of these.

I dedicate *Nog vele jaren* to my children: Merel, Esther, Liesbeth, Judith, and Anna—in trust.

Hans Korteweg

## PERSONAL COMMENTARY

I didn't consider this before I began, but it is of course inevitable that by writing a book about the whole of life one is constantly going to be confronted with one's own life. With each year I described, the memories of my past and expectations for my future came to the surface, and I had to detach them from my writing. I wanted to write a book about the lives of all people, not a generalized version of my own life story. Nevertheless, I did test my words constantly against my experiences and against my vision of what the rest of my life will bring. That had a remarkable effect on me and made the book all the more real for me.

It gradually dawned on me that, although this book may not be an abstracted history of my life, it is still a subjective book. It is the fruit of a certain way of living and a certain way of looking and thinking. It is a book with a history—the history of my relationship with numbers and symbols.

I want to say something about that.

## QUALITIES & QUANTITIES

As a child I heard many fairy tales. My mother read them to me along with biblical stories, which she also regarded as fairy tales. She had not been raised as a Christian, and so for her the Bible was free of any religious baggage when she first encountered it as an adult. I loved the beautiful stories she told me, and when I became older, I began to read them for myself. Those fairy tales were a reality for me. In today's language, they were an inner reality. They provided me with the inner food that helped me to grow up and feel the connections between things in a very natural way. Fairy tales and biblical stories teem with numbers. We read about the seven fat and seven lean years, the seven days of creation, the seven dwarves, the seven little goats; the three brothers who go out into the world to find the water of life for their father, the three bears, the three sisters (One-eye, Two-eyes, and Three-eyes), the trinity consisting of God, Jesus, and the Holy Ghost; the twelve brothers who turn into ravens, the twelve disciples, the twelve tribes of Israel, and so on. In one way or another,

these numbers were just as important to me as the things they stood for. It was as if the number were the surname and what was being counted bore the given name, so that in my imagination, the little goats, the fat and the lean years, and the days of creation belonged to the same family—the family of seven. There were a lot of these families, innumerable ones, from zero to a million.

In retrospect, I can now say that in my early youth I got to know the numbers as animated things—living beings—that represented an emotional value. I suppose that everybody is aware of this value—I quite often hear that people have favorite numbers and consider numbers in the first place as qualities. I know I certainly did. It was only later at grammar school that I came to see them as quantities—symbols that represent certain quantities, like apples or pears—and as a means to carry out calculations. As a child, I was very good at doing sums and perhaps the reason was that, unlike other children, I did not have to learn the numbers by heart; they already existed in my heart.

Gradually at primary school, the quantitative took over the qualitative. I took in more and more information, and my imagination retreated. Numbers became ciphers—the marks I earned from my homework, the amount of pocket money I received from my father. But I still read fairy tales occasionally, and sometimes, in the midst of all the other things I was busy with, I found myself drawing a pentagon, and inside it a pentagon, and in that another pentagon, even smaller and smaller. Then, it was there again, that feeling of contact. I did not know then that the great Greek mathematicians and philosophers like Pythagoras saw numbers as supreme entities and as the beginning of the whole of creation. I did not realize that there were cultures to whom my way of handling numbers was completely natural and in which every number—birthdate, year, number of children—was seen firstly as a quality, an expression of a deeper reality.

Years later I found this nicely illustrated by an event that took place in China during a war. Eleven generals came together to decide whether they should retreat or attack. After they had talked about this for a long time, they voted. Eight were in favor of retreating; the other three were in favor of attacking. They decided unanimously to attack, because three was the number of agreement. The story ends by saying that the attack was a great success.

## THE GOOSEBOARD

Through primary school and secondary school, I found the subject of mathematics very dry. I detested it until, in my sixteenth year, I discovered the great book of wisdom, the *I Ching*. There they were again: the numbers and rhythmical patterns, a wealth of beautiful images, and a language that I understood intuitively but could not follow logically. A few years later I came across the "game of life"—the Tarot—with its seventy-eight cards. In the following years I regularly consulted the *I Ching*, laid the Tarot, and looked at the cards, but that was all until I turned twenty-five. Then, as I was tidying up a few things one day, I found an old children's game in a box. It was the old Dutch game of gooseboard, a board game in which goose-shaped pieces are moved along a path spiraling toward the center. Along this path, players encounter obstacles at certain numbers, a well at thirty-one, for example, at which some penalty must be paid. This board game fascinated me. I could see it now as I had never seen it before, as if I were seeing it for the first time.

I played it a few times, alone and with others. It was quite nice, but not much more than that—it is not exactly an exciting game. Yet it haunted me. I frequently caught myself thinking about the combination of numbers and symbols: What did thirty-one have to do with the well? Why was the end marked sixty-three? It began to dawn on me that this game, just like the Tarot, was a game of life, and that the symbols (bridge, inn, well, maze, prison, and death) represented the obstacles on the path of life. I started to draw the game of goose in my own way, using the spiral form, the numbers, and the symbols.

Now I was really under its spell and decided to write an article about the origins of the game. Although it took me a long time to put what I knew intuitively into words, I never tired of the subject; it still fascinated me. As I worked on the article, once more I saw the numbers as the surnames around which images and symbols arranged themselves. I began to realize that the "family" of a certain number represented a particular quality, and I did my utmost to give this quality a name. I made whole lists of numbers and the places where I encountered them—in myths and fairy tales and the great books of humankind. I saw that while different cultures associated different symbols and images with the same number, I could find similarities and connections among them. For instance, the number forty-two is the maze in the game of goose; in the *Egyptian Book of the Dead*, there are forty-two gods that one has to call on—by their secret names—if one wants to enter the realm of eternal life; the Jews encountered forty-two resting places during their wanderings in the desert; when the Greek hero Theseus conquered the Minotaur it had already devoured forty-two young men. The similarity I saw was that in all these sources, the number forty-two had something to do with a quest through a maze—the search for the Promised Land, so to speak—in which the maze represents the material world of space and time.

Working on in this way, I found a concept for every number that plays a part in the game of goose. I was then faced with the next question—if the game of goose is, as I assumed it to be, a game of life, then do these numbers also correspond with people's ages? For instance, does the year of the maze and the quest through the maze begin at our forty-second birthday?

I answered this question with a provisional yes. I could see many parallels between age and the symbolic meanings of numbers, but I was still asking myself whether this was accidental or a pointer to a deeper connection. I left it at that. I finished my article and had the good fortune to see it immediately published in a magazine.

## COSMIC PATTERNS

A few years later, in 1970, I wrote a book about the archetypal patterns (as I had now come to call the underlying reality of myths, symbols, and numbers) in the astrology of the Indians and Chinese, among others. Once more the numbers came back, this time connected with astrological symbols such as the sun, moon, Jupiter, and Saturn. One could say that the book was about the astrological children in the families of one, three, seven, and twelve. Moreover, it was a book about time, cyclic patterns in time, and the effect these have upon our ways of thinking and feeling.

According to astrologists, the planets have a direct effect upon our lives, beyond the simple effect of the one cosmic "mark" with which we are stamped at birth. The effect of this astrological "birthmark" is felt over and over throughout our lives. The birthmark is activated again and again by the sun, the moon, and the planets, especially when a planet or a light (the sun or moon) has returned to the point where it stood at the time of our birth. Every planet and every

light has its own cycle; for example, Jupiter takes twelve years to return to its starting point, whereas Uranus takes eighty-four years.

It takes the sun, as seen from Earth, a little over 365 days to return to its starting point—that is our year. Our birthday occurs when the sun is in exactly the same position as it was when we were born. The unit of one year is, for everyone on Earth, a fundamental fact. In the course of a year we go through four seasons; we experience many phases of light and darkness.

Through studying these cosmic patterns, I came to understand that a year is a real unit and that the number associated with each year—our age—is not just the expression of a quantity, but also of a quality.

## A GENIUS WITH NUMBERS

At about this time, I received a bundle of notes about numbers from a friend. He had come across them in the legacy of a person I didn't know. These notes proved to be invaluable for me, even though it took me more than twenty years to fully understand them. This stranger to me was a true genius in the field of numbers. Even though I can now understand what he had written, I still feel as if I am a wren riding on the back of an eagle.

I understood right away the notes on prime numbers (numbers that can only be divided by themselves or by one, for example, three or thirty-seven). The notes contained a short description of the meaning of all of these prime numbers, up to and including 127. One might say that the prime numbers are the only real numbers and that all other numbers are a combination of one or more prime numbers. So the number forty-two, for instance, is a combination of two, three, and seven ($42 = 2 \times 3 \times 7$). Viewed this way, the number forty-two is a product of the symbols two, three, and seven. In other words, the pattern of two, the pattern of three, and the pattern of seven meet each other in forty-two. The multiplication tables of prime numbers show us the patterns that exist in the world of numbers—that is to say, in the archetypal world.

In the years that followed, I applied what I knew about numbers to the ages of people I knew. Sometimes I wrote a portrait of what a particular year had in store for a friend, symbolically speaking. It was fun to do, and the people I did it for seemed to enjoy it. In those years, then, I was testing archetypal reality against daily practice.

## THE ARCHETYPAL AGE

I come now to the end of my story. In the last few years, I have written a number of books about spiritual psychology, with the help of some others. The crowning glory of my work was a book I wrote with Hanneke Korteweg-Frankhuisen and Jaap Voight about growth and initiation, *The Great Leap: About Growth and Initiation* (Utrecht: Netherlands: Servire, Cothen, 1990). This book explains how it is possible to awaken spiritually in this existence, which is confined by time and space. The emphasis lies on the saltatory, or abrupt awakening. When this book was finished, my interest in numbers and the way they relate to each other returned suddenly. I decided to write a book about the life of a human being, giving a description of each year. At the same time, I wanted to write a sort of companion volume to *The Great Leap,* indicating how life in space and time gives us the opportunity to become a whole human being—year on year. I sorted out all of the material I had and was immediately faced with the following question: If I am to write about the life of a human being, how long is a human's life-span? Do I use the average life expectancy? Do I stop at seventy-two or at eighty? I dropped the idea of the average age right away—I was not interested in an average life; I was interested in life's potential. I wanted to describe what life can be when heaven and earth—the archetypal reality and the reality of space and time—come together in a human being. The question was not, what is the life expectancy of the average human being? but rather, what is the life expectancy of the archetypal human being?

There is no absolute answer to that question. There is no such thing as an archetypal encyclopedia in which one can find the definite answer to this type of question. One can choose from a certain number of possibilities between sixty-five and one hundred (of these, sixty-five, seventy, seventy-two, eighty, eighty-four,

and one hundred seemed to be the most obvious choices, as far as I was concerned). One makes a personal choice out of these possibilities. In the end I chose the age of eighty-four. The major life cycles of three and four come together at this respectable age (I'll return to this in the general commentary). At eighty-four, twelve phases of seven years have been completed: twelve is the number of "being in time," times seven, the number of "loving creation." At eighty-four, one is four times an adult, or to put that in an archetypal way, the four cycles or "seasons" of life have been fulfilled. (I will discuss this further in the general commentary at the end of this book.) Seen from an astrological point of view, eighty-four is seven times the cycle of Jupiter or one time the cycle of Uranus. At age eighty-four, the maze is right in the middle of existence. Much more could be said about this, but I will leave it for now.

So, from the archetypal point of view, I have set the life span of a human being at eighty-four years. I hope it is obvious that I am not implying that there is no need to grow older than eighty-four years or that you can become a complete human being only by reaching that age.

Once I had defined the life span I would describe, I started to work the material I had gathered on the years zero to eighty-four into miniature portraits. Immediately, the next problem presented itself. I realized that I had to be very careful not to write a spiritual "cookbook." I could write about possibilities, about archetypal patterns and stimuli, but what I wrote wouldn't have an objective, binding truth. This book is *not* a cookbook, nor is it a code of law. I describe archetypal influences, not results. Human beings turn influences into results. The archetypal as such does not have a final form. It takes on a certain form because a human being responds to it in a particular way.

For example, I call the period between forty-two and sixty-three the autumn of life. This general truth of human life doesn't say anything about the way people will see themselves at this time or how they will behave. Just as it is with the autumn we all go through each year, one person

may respond to the "falling leaves" with despair, while another responds with a feeling of joy and elation. The personal response one makes to the archetypal impulse is the determining factor. And for me it goes one step further: only by making a personal response to the questions and stimuli of life does one become the person that one really is.

With this motto, which should also act as a warning to the reader, I have come to the end of my personal story. All that remains is to give a general exposé of the numerical rhythms that underlie the patterns of the years, which I have done in the general commentary at the end of this book.

*The First Period*
*0 to 28*
*Developing the Personality*

## THE FIRST PHASE
## 0 TO 7 YEARS
## COMING FROM HEAVEN

Here are the first shoots of human life. Coming from the unknown, the child arrives on Earth. Giving her a name, her parents call her *their* child, but in the beginning, she is more a child of the *oneness* of creation than of the world of duality. She doesn't yet recognize herself as *I*. She doesn't yet distinguish herself from her surroundings.

The child is completely dependent on his surroundings for his needs—food, warmth, love, and so on. Without the aid of his surroundings, he would soon die.

After a while, the first *I* awareness begins to develop. The child becomes shy, self-conscious; she begins to develop a certain character. No longer continually embedded in *unity*, the child leaves paradise.

In this time, the child has grown considerably. He has learned an enormous amount: he can walk and talk, he is toilet trained, and he has developed some practical skills. The child has an insatiable thirst for knowledge. In no other period of life does so much happen than in these first seven years.

The child is now ready to enter the world.

*0 to 7 Coming from Heaven*

## 0  First Birth

*Coming from light*

*Entering light*

*Baby*

*We give you*

*A name*

*You know nothing*

*Knowing everything*

*0 to 7 Coming from Heaven*

1 *Many, many years, just like this one!*

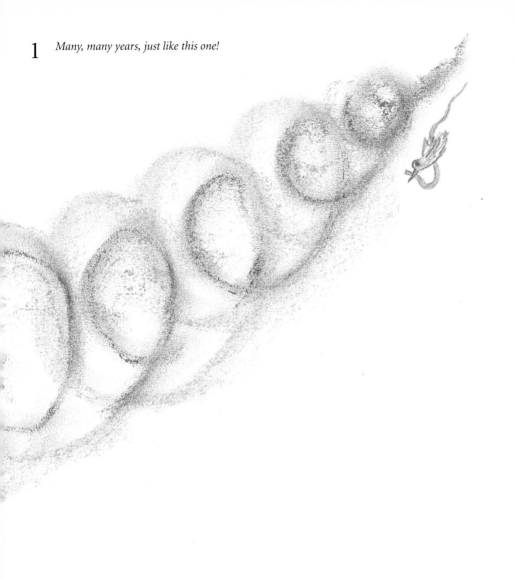

2 *Mommy Daddy Me*

*Good Ow Yes Bah*

*Naughty No Mmm Nice*

*Home*

*Bed*

*0 to 7 Coming from Heaven*

**3**  *Adventure!*

*Leaving the familiar street,*

*Looking around—so much to see!*

*I can do that!*

*Carry me!*

*I don't like that!*

*Can I have ice cream?*

*I want ice cream!*

*I have to have ice cream now!!*

*I want to go to sleep now*

*On your lap.*

*Tell me a story.*

*Nice.*

3 is the creative child. Expectant and apprehensive, he shows himself, he hides; he loses, he finds.

Exploring yes and no, she learns about duality. In the process of learning, she will find her own unique form of expression.

*0 to 7 Coming from Heaven*

4

*Where are we now?*
*Where are we going?*
*Whyyyyyy?*

*How many eyes has a monkey got,*
*When it's sitting on the back of a*
*sheep?*

*Summer, winter,*
*Autumn, spring.*
*Morning, afternoon,*
*Evening, night.*
*Front and back,*
*Top and bottom.*

*One, two, three, four, ten!*
*Ready or not, here I come!*

*0 to 7 Coming from Heaven*

4 is the perceivable world.
4 is the game of life in a nutshell.
The basis of personality is laid
down. The first lines of personal
destiny are drawn. The game can
begin.

4 is still in the dreamtime, yet he is
already taking on his form in space
and time.

**5** *Mirror mirror on the wall,*
*Who's the fairest one of all?*
*(or the ugliest, nicest, stupidest,*
*strongest, loveliest, funniest . . .)*

4 could feel shame; 5 adds guilt to shame. What was natural and self-evident now breaks into two parts: good and bad.

5 wakes up—wide awake! She sits up and looks around. She plays with what she sees, without thought, endlessly interested. Suddenly she stops and asks herself: "What did I just do? Why did I do that?"

Innocence looks at innocence, and, in playing, leaves paradise. 5 looks at itself and sees that it is a boy or a girl.

5 is clear intelligence, observing outside and within himself.
5 begins to discover himself, comparing with others.

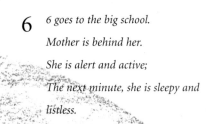

**6** *6 goes to the big school.*
*Mother is behind her.*
*She is alert and active;*
*The next minute, she is sleepy and*
*listless.*

He learns about numbers
and lines and letters.
He dreams of undulating colors.
At the border between waking and
dreaming, he likes to hear stories
with happy endings
(though they may be frightening,
just for a moment).

6 is small *and* big.
6 is completely alive
(and sometimes, in the evening,
just a *little* bit frightened of dying).

*0 to 7 Coming from Heaven*

## THE SECOND PHASE
## 7 TO 14 YEARS
## ALL THIS THAT I AM

The child learns to know himself from all sides. He grows in all senses of the word, finds real friends (male and female), and belongs to a group or a club or a gang. He begins to develop a clear-cut personality.

By the end of this period, the child has really grown, but with growth comes the feeling that she is pushing against the limits of her world. She is still in contact, emotionally, with the place of *oneness* from which she originated, but she finds that space, time, and the discoveries she is continually making in this space-time demand virtually all her attention.

*7 to 14 All This That I Am*

The Jesuits used to say that if only they could supervise a child's upbringing through the seventh year, it didn't matter what happened to the child after that age.

During the first seven years, the dough is mixed, kneaded, placed in the baking tray. At 7 it is put into the oven—for the next seven years.

The child is now really ready for school. He gathers information greedily. Knowledge increases, and a certain distance begins to form between the mental and emotional worlds. Almost every child will move in one of two directions at this age—the way of feeling or the way of thinking; the way of love or the way of wisdom. Later in life, every person will have the task of welding these two together again. The result will be something new: love-wisdom.

You could say that at 7 there is a separation of father and mother; not the worldly father and mother, but rather the inner, *archetypal* father and mother. These represent two very different approaches to life: a mental approach, attempting to answer life's many riddles, and an emotional approach, going with the flow of life.

When this separation happens, the child will go with one or the other. Later in life, the adult may find out how to bring "father and mother" back together. If this task—what the alchemists called the "great work"—is completed successfully, then he will possess the ability to think with the heart and feel with the mind.

**8** The head and heart separation that begins at 7 becomes problematic at 8. 8 is the number of tension and stress: tension between above and below, tension between unbridled energy and life's rules and regulations, tension between male and female. The child begins to take her own place in the world. She develops a certain stubbornness. She grows more angular, coming more regularly into collision with her environment.

Friendships grow and fade, groups form, and leaders emerge, competing for position. At 8, the first signs of a more visible social order are revealed.

At 8, puberty seems to be starting already, but it is only a finger exercise for what will come later.

**9** 9 is the year of the *brandmark*. Life is like a mother, watching over her children from beginning to end. She sees their distinguishing marks, she sees where they belong. She distinguishes the doers from the dreamers, the speakers from the healers, the builders from the destroyers. She distinguishes the true family of every child.

To each of her children, she sends a sign. In this sign, the child recognizes his destiny. The sign may come during the day or at night in a dream. This sign is the *brandmark*.

The branding happens like a lightning flash, illuminating instantaneously his whole world. When the shock of it has passed, forgetfulness takes over or the whole event is explained away as if it were something more mundane. Later in life, as head and heart converge again, he will remember when he was touched by the hand of life and the brandmark it left behind.

*7 to 14 All This That I Am*

10　The child knows herself: This is me; that isn't me. I would never do that. I will tell you this; I will not tell you that. Some things are hidden in a secret place in her mind. She begins to define her individuality against the outside world.

The secret place begins to lead a life of its own. It becomes a dark cave that, after a time, she fears to enter. Still later, she will avoid that dark place as something dangerous.

Sometimes she will play near the edge of the cave, in the shadow of it, with a friend, male or female. To do that is both exciting and frightening—this is where adventures are had and stories are told.

Who knows? When she has grown up, she may return to this cave.

**11** It is strength—a flood of vitality. Girls are girls and boys are boys, and ne'er the twain shall meet.

The bonds and friendships made earlier are now broken; specialization increases; individuality develops further.

11 is the year of trust and betrayal, of deceit and honesty, of togetherness and aloneness. The way is prepared for future lives as social beings and for the laws that govern social lives.

11 is stronger than his surroundings allow him to be; others still see him as weak. His energy urges him to do more than his physical form will yet allow, which creates considerable difficulties.

11 doesn't know what to do with this newfound energy, so the energy looks for ways out and finds them in prattling, mischief making, tale telling, teasing, fighting. In control and out of control, 11 learns to make friends with his energy.

**12**

The unfettered energy of 11 finds its limitations in 12.

The descent into the world is now complete; 12 has become a fully fledged child of time and space.

12 can move in every direction; she can look forward and she can look back. She is *grown,* and having grown, she finds herself pushing at the boundaries of her world. Emotionally, she is still in contact with the world of unity she came from, but space and time and the discoveries she makes in those realms absorb nearly all her attention.

12 is trying to wrap the ball of original knowledge up in the cube of daily awareness. This causes friction and she doesn't understand why.

She experiences that something she possesses one moment can be lost the next. The more she becomes a child of time, the more she understands what it means to lose. In learning how to lose, she really starts to grow up.

If she can't cope with loss, she will be confronted with all sorts of problems. By wanting to always win, she holds desperately to a sort of pseudo-unity in which everything revolves around herself. She doesn't have the power to hold this pseudo-unity together for long.

12 has to learn that she doesn't hold all the cards in her hands, no matter how big and strong she feels she is. 12 needs to learn to accept, and particularly to accept loss. This may seem like an enormous step to make at this age, but it is a necessary condition for the development of individuality and the beginning of experiential wisdom.

# 13

13 is the beginning of the new. For the conservatively inclined, 13 is an unlucky number. On the other hand, those who love life know that progress comes through death and renewal, through rebirth. 13 is the ending of the old, as well as the phoenix that rises from its ashes.

At 13, we take stock of life up until now.

Parents and friends are put to the test once more. This leads to friction and struggle, because 13 can be so undiplomatic, even cruel. Upbringing can do little to remove this obstacle because 13 can't be "brought up" any further. Others get along with him or they don't, and that's that. If others want to get along with him, they can oppose him or stand next to him, but they cannot stand above him. 13 is a little adult, with his own consciences.

13 is lively, arrogant, full of initiative.

# THE THIRD PHASE
# 14 TO 21 YEARS
# THE WHEEL TURNS

In this phase, contradictions come to the fore. It is marked by inner struggle and struggle with our environment. The wheel of life turns; what was below is now above, resulting in a complete reorientation. Head fights with heart; the thinker becomes a feeler, the feeler a thinker.

Our own values and norms emerge. The family is left behind. Our destiny becomes visible in our contact with others. Sexuality becomes active. We begin to see people as girls and boys, men and women. We explore, discover, or retreat and lock ourselves up. Our attitudes toward our own sex and the other may be determined for life during this phase. When the wheel stops turning at the end of this phase, we feel relieved. We command a view of the world and can say, "So this is what it's all about."

## 14

What's done, what isn't done? Where do I fit in, where don't I fit in?

At 14 there is a severe schism between us and our families. Criticism is particularly directed at those who were up until recently the two great examples: our mothers and fathers.

"Vertical" relationships break up more and more; "horizontal" relationships take their place. Male and female friends are our new examples; we test ourselves against them now. But at 14 we don't really find a place of rest in our peer groups because we aren't really just one age. One moment we are much older; the next, much younger. One moment we are as affectionate as children; the next, detached and "adult."

*14 to 21 The Wheel Turns*

So much is still unclear, and there are so many possibilities—the subjects of our fantasies—that we find it hard to keep to one role. Yet, being as critical as we are, we will feel ashamed in an instant if we fall out of the self-chosen role of the moment.

Head fights heart. Unrelenting criticism and self-criticism exist on one side, flaring emotions on the other. Sexual development simply adds fuel to the fire.

Nothing is certain anymore. Even your face in the mirror changes from day to day. And nobody, absolutely nobody understands how radiantly beautiful, how hideously ugly you think yourself to be.

# 15

15 is like Sleeping Beauty. We want to spin our own life's thread, to take our fate in our own hands. But since we are still so inexperienced at life, the inevitable result is self-inflicted pain and injury. Parents long to spare their children this pain, but they discover that it is impossible to watch over us at all times. Thank God! We must find our own way, and part of that process will be walking into problems that are all our own and "falling asleep" in our own unique way.

15 grows in willfulness—we develop our own very distinct opinions. But at the same time, we lose something—the feeling of being embedded in oneness. It is this feeling of oneness that falls into a deep sleep.

Try as they might, our parents can't wake us from this sleep. That honor is reserved for someone from beyond the family walls: that "fairy tale" prince or princess—the life partner who may (or may not) one day walk into our lives.

15 hears the world saying that everything has two sides. It says that we will have to choose from those two sides. It is yes or no, on or off, fun or work. You can't have your cake *and* eat it! Toss a coin—it's heads or tails.

15 says that a coin may roll and roll—it doesn't *have* to fall one way or another. We don't believe in the "this-or-that" theory. 15 goes in search of the third way. *Freedom* is our key word.

Nobody is allowed to choose for us. We aren't going to let this world of unending possibilities be reduced to a choice between this or that. We fight for our freedom. Our motto is

I am unique.
I am
the way I am:
and just a bit different!

## 16 Sweet sixteen?
Bitter, sweet, sour, salty sixteen!

No taste is missed. At 16 we show ourselves every corner of our inner world, although nobody else is aware of it.

The brandmark that we received when we were 9 is felt now. We start looking around ourselves for our "real family." Recognizing is part of falling in love, part of passionate friendship.

Walking an endless tightrope between pain and joy, 16 searches for freedom but finds limitation. At 16, we find that we are also who we don't want to be.

Patterns recur. 16 walks into the same things time and again. Fate becomes visible in our contact with other people.

# 17

Can it be that an end is in sight to this seemingly eternal tension and conflict?

In any case, there is now a greater receptivity to something beyond the emotional. A star appears in the heavens.

Amid all the excitement, there is a point of stillness, a deep knowing certainty. Wisdom and love approach each other. To use the language of myth, the Greater Mother takes 17 into her bosom, comforting and protecting. She wraps her garment around her children, letting us know that we are not alone in all of this experience, that our experiences are embedded in a cosmos breathing with love.

At 17, we still feel that we don't belong among the regularity of the "established ways." We remain critical, but this criticism becomes less defensive, more the development of our own perspective.

**18** The battle is not over yet! Now, the polarity of man and woman comes into the spotlight.

Life has two faces—it also has two bodies. 18 wonders, what am I looking for? Am I being looked for? Am I wanted? What kind of man, what sort of woman am I?

Just as 3 began to move into the world, hesitantly, in a unique way, so 18 hesitantly begins to find a way of approaching "the other." If hesitancy is lacking, then the *own way* is usually lacking too.

If we don't dare to find our own way to approach others, complications and negative patterns develop that may be irreversible. These complications, both with our own and with the opposite sex, will recur throughout life. The only way out is to become 18 once more and, meeting another eye-to-eye, hesitantly find our own way. The period between 25 and 42 is one time when we are confronted again with what we thought we could avoid at 18.

# 19

19 is a time of activity. Destiny is seen in a new light.

The high seas of emotion are beginning to calm, and new land comes into view.

At 17, the connection to the Great Mother was restored; at 19, it is the Father principle that is readmitted. The Father principle is less romantic, less poetic, more concrete, and geared toward doing. The Great Mother enfolds and heals; the Great Father gives powerful impetus and points to the beginning of the individual life path.

At 19 we are no longer children. Our natural fathers and mothers now entrust us to life. If we want to stay a child and cling to our parents, we will grow no further than this, becoming no more than copies of our fathers or mothers, repeating their patterns.

What we fail to do between 14 and 21 to please our parents will hinder us when we come to join the greater family of society between 21 and 28, and will return as the Minotaur in the "labyrinth of existence" between 42 and 49.

If we let our vital impulses lead us rather than our family bonds, we have become an adult—a radiating focus.

**20** 20 finds self among forms. The world becomes our house. 20 juggles with possibilities—and contradictions. When we drop something, we know the art of pretending that we did it on purpose. This is an enjoyable game.

We have our own place among a circle of friends and acquaintances. We make connections and develop relationships. We build our world. We look at what is going on around us; bring people, things, ideas together; let something new emerge. In the true sense, we are acting with intelligence.

We infuse the forms and patterns of the world around us with our individuality. The dwellers in the world of fixed forms and patterns aren't always too happy about that.

20 has experienced much in the last few years. You have been spun around like a top. Now you have landed on your feet again; you oversee your world and say: "Aha! That's the way it is."

## THE FOURTH PHASE
## 21 TO 28 YEARS
## ALONE AND TOGETHER

In the fourth phase, we say good-bye to our earlier peer groups. Deeper personal friendships, love relationships, and more complex social contacts come in their place. The relationship with the first group we belonged to—our family—becomes important again.

We develop further and continue to learn. We have become people, we have our own opinions and directions in life. We experiment with our talents, doing this and that, but who we really are still eludes us. We are still apprentices to life.

At the end of this period, the phase of personality development is over. We have grown up.

**21**

Between 14 and 21, a group formed that you belonged to. There may even have been several groups, each representing a different aspect of your developing personality.

In this phase that is now beginning, you leave these groups behind, and deeper personal friendships, more wide-ranging social contacts, come in their place.

In addition, your relationship with the first group in your life—your family—becomes important again.

Society sees 21 as an adult, with rights and responsibilities. There is no longer anyone standing protectively between us and the world.

We are individuals who stand alone against society's patterns, laws, and regulations, the fruits of the collective past. Either we contribute creatively to these patterns or we adapt ourselves to them. This is the process that starts at 21.

In essence, you are a new idea, a new substance to be mixed in with the old substance that, like yeast, sets in motion a process that can lead to the transformation of the whole mixture. You are something that has never before existed.

If 21 dares to stand alone, to lose and playfully find identity again, then the all-important transition period that happens at 30 will be passed through without much trouble.

*21 to 28 Alone and Together*

22 says, "I will invest my energy here, but not there." If you don't choose now, you will lose yourself in fragmentation.

All ingredients of life are ready. The only question is, what are you going to do with them? If you do nothing, if you don't deal with life in your own way, if you don't write your own story with the material that you now have, you will be swamped by the multiplicity of it all. You will feel torn and helpless, a nothing.

22 has to learn to bundle our energies and express them in one straightforward way. If we can do that, bundling our talents and offering them to the world in a certain form, we will no longer feel worthless.

22 is a crisis year, although in a totally different way than 14 and 42 are. While the crises at those ages are crises of being, 22 presents a crisis of possession. The question here is, will we hold back everything we have gathered, keeping it for ourselves, or will we share it, passing it on in our own way?

If 22 gets stuck, it is out of a mixture of selfishness and pride. We sit on our talents and knowledge for too long, waiting for the moment when we think we have perfected them.

The creative energy that is liberated at 22 asks that we use it. To use it, we must make sacrifices. Here, personal growth occurs through an influx of energy.

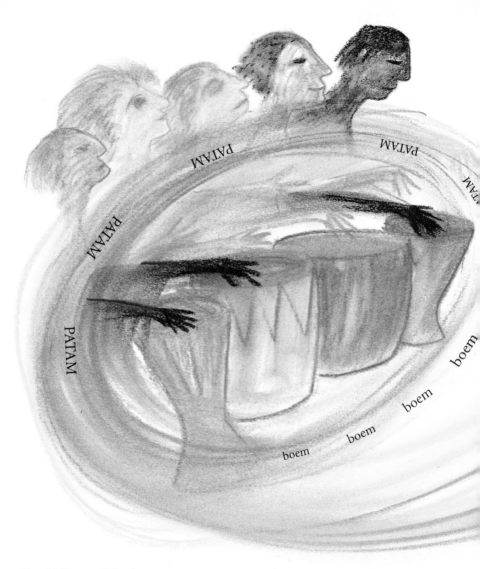

*21 to 28 Alone and Together*

**23** All knowledge is useless if it isn't connected to the rhythm that vibrates through everything. Knowledge is bare and fruitless without the cadence of life.

Rhythm wakes you, starts you moving, takes you beyond the borders of the known. Such is life. Knowledge moves from the head downward; rhythm from the feet up. Where rhythm and knowledge meet, there emerges the living word.

To speak the truth, let yourself be moved with everything you know.

23 is opened. Standing in the open, on the plain of life, you no longer mimic what others say; you begin to speak your own language.

23 follows the rhythm, leaving behind what stands in rhythm's way. Your attachments and habits become clear.

Is freedom possible? Patam patam patam!

**24** Love finds limitation and becomes very personal. It is easy enough to love all people everywhere; it is much more to love one special person. 24 experiences what it means to make love concrete in daily life and what must be sacrificed for it.

Everything that was developed as ego structure in the first four years of life comes into discussion. Old fears return; doubts that you thought you had overcome long ago raise their heads again. This does not happen because there is any justification in those doubts or because the fears refer to anything in particular, but because the experience of love reactivates these old bugbears. With so much light, what was invisible in darker days can again be made out.

24 becomes wise. We learn that frustration and limitation are paths to self-knowledge.

**25** You find again and again that your world has also become the world of another. This happens because you allow the other to enter too far into your territory and because you make yourself dependent. It is seductive to think that someone else knows who you really are, what your destiny is, what you have to do.

25 sees clearly that we can bring our world to life only when we see where we are dependent and then take action to break out of that dependence. We see that no one else can set us free and that we must follow our own intuition and our own knowledge. When we follow our inspiration, we uncover a trail. We think that trail was always there, but this isn't so. It comes into being when we take a step beyond what our needs for security and organization were dependent upon. If we look further than the end of our noses, out of curiosity and in faith, we may make contact with our good genius.

This guardian angel, so naturally present in the first years of life, can now be rediscovered as a light force in day-to-day events. The trail that 25 creates with good genius eventually leads beyond the limits of personality toward a spiritual maturity.

**26** 26 is about steady growth and the application of new values. 26 is about finding some peace within.

In an atmosphere of togetherness, everything that has been gained over the last few years can now be tested in daily practice.

26 is about strengthening and deepening.

26 develops the quality of devotion. We learn how to be faithful to the smaller details of life, to not look for big results. The effect that we have on others and the results of our own actions escape us.

These results often have little to do with our original intentions. This realization doesn't distract from our enthusiasm, but it also doesn't add to our modesty. It *may* make us into more receptive partners, friends, or colleagues.

# 27

27 is like someone who has circumnavigated the world and is now approaching the point from which he first departed.

We have experienced much on this journey; we have seen everything there was to be seen (although we may not have explored it in as much detail as we'd have liked—there was always the pressure to move on), but generally speaking, we now know our world.

We can converse on just about any subject; we know that there are areas we want to explore more deeply; we also know that there are areas we have avoided for one reason or another during our first journey or passed by in our sleep.

We can map out all of these areas. We can resolve to pay extra attention to some of these areas on our new journey, which starts the moment we get back to our starting places.

27 is, in a way, the point before zero—right before birth.

Since our first birth, we have become somebody, become something. As this somebody, this something—with a name, a family history, an education, a personality, friends, lovers, colleagues—we enter a new cycle.

27 finishes what has been started. We see what we have done so far with our talents.

We can now recognize the ups and downs of our lives as being *our* patterns. Everything is now spread out before us.

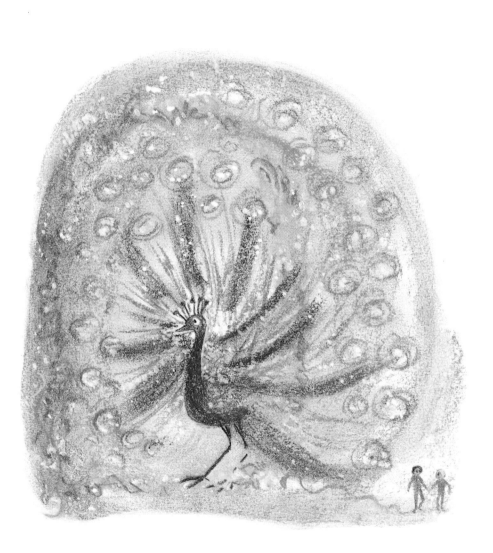

*The Second Period*
*28 to 56*
*Becoming an Individual*

## THE FIFTH PHASE
## 28 TO 35 YEARS
## ENTERING THE WORLD

The fifth phase involves entering life to the full. The apprenticeship is over, and we realize that each of us has a unique task in life.

New urges or stimuli, possibly resulting in drastic changes, will have to be assimilated, especially at the beginning of this period. These impulses will have to be worked out in the world at large, in contrast to similar impulses at puberty, which were worked out in the private sphere.

In this phase, we express ourselves, searching for our own styles. We wrestle free from old styles and leave them behind.

Ease of mind and certainty of direction come gradually, as does our way in society.

A new period begins at 28. It is characterized by a reorientation that can lead to a transformation of the personality that was formed in the first twenty-eight years.

In this new period, the personality can become an individual, fulfilling a unique destiny. In this way, we can make our contribution to the world.

The seeds of promise are already present at 28. It is a hopeful prognosis.

But the personality doesn't experience it in such a positive way because, for the personality, 28 is a crisis point. The labor pains that come with this second birth cannot be avoided.

It is strange that the crisis around age 28 is so less well known than the one around age 14 (puberty) and that around 42 (the midlife crisis). At 28, the personality has to deal with very strong impulses, which often leads to drastic change. Perhaps this is because the revolution that happens at 28 is not directed against authority (as against the parents at puberty) and does not form a threat to the established order (as it does during the midlife crisis). Our worldly position, the way we function in the world, isn't threatened.

At 28, the realization dawns that
we have a unique task in life. This
realization is often covered up by
feelings of guilt and powerlessness.
At 28, we are aware of what we have
left undone so far in our lives, what
we cannot leave undone, and what
we must let go of in order to fulfill
our destinies.

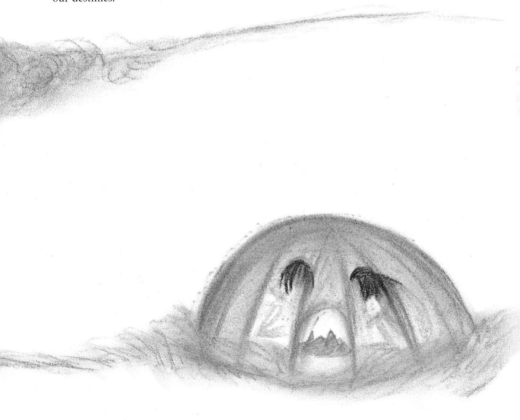

**29** Within the crisis period, this is a year of choice. We decide what we want to work on and with whom, as well as what general direction we want to give our lives.

Feelings of suffocation and self-judgmental thoughts may be very strong at this time, but the new self that is developing is also strong and takes little interest in worries, emotions, and doubts. In the middle of so much subjectivity, an objective force awakens. From time to time, we encounter the enormous potential that humans are connected to, a potential that is very rarely used. We experience periods of great creative energy and insight. At these times, if we have any sort of visionary ability, we are allowed a bird's-eye view of our whole life—light and dark, suffering and happiness—and we see how it is all inseparably connected.

Whatever happens, in this year you will meet with forces that you had thought you would be able to shut out of your life. These forces, which actually are talents that you hadn't yet integrated into your personality, now break through into your life and are responsible for some surprises.

You will have to review the image you had of yourself. Once you have done that, you will see that these forces aren't enemies, but allies.

**30** The crisis of self-expression continues. This year, it focuses on the tension between personality and essence, between *I* and *self.*

For most people, there is a big difference between who they really are on the inside and how they behave on the outside. If their behavior (the personality mask) blocks out the sound of their inner voice (the essence), then the mask will find itself under enormous pressure this year. The essence is not satisfied with weak-willed interpretations of reality and compromises; it seeks expression, even when the personality resists expression. Slips of the tongue, mistakes of all sorts, outbursts, embarrassing scenes, comical situations are all the result.

In this period, the personality has the opportunity to learn that it isn't a product of the personal environment or, in the wider sense, of society. It is an instrument whose main purpose is to serve the essence, the self. It is the personality's role to give shape and form to the inspiration that comes from the self. It should pass on what the self wishes to have passed on, even if it can't foresee the consequences. If the personality takes on too strongly the role of the censor, censoring and selecting the wishes of the self, then creativity is impossible and mediocrity will be the result.

30 has a choice: revelation or repression.

If we choose repression, adapting to the environment and over-developing the personality mask, our next opportunity to discover our real self will be ten to fifteen years later—during the midlife crisis.

# 31

31 is the year of the solution. The tension that has been building up for so long is now either released and transformed into something unique or buried in the deepest hole you can find. Whichever way, fundamental choices will be made.

The crisis isn't totally over, but the sharpest edges are now softened.

This year, we can feel once more that life gives and takes, and that we are protected from all sides. There is room for thankfulness.

In these last few years, the heart, deeply wounded although few of us have realized it, has gradually been released from its painful captivity. Heart and mind have drawn closer together.

Although we often lose sight of the big picture, we have now learned to honor the small, and in so doing, we can climb out of the pit.

32 There are many possibilities, but nobody else knows what is best for you. That is the recurring theme of this year. You can get lost in endless doubt or become a Ping-Pong ball for the sake of your environment. Either way leads to further splintering.

32 stands still and asks the heart for advice, looking for essence in many things. This is a risk—essence always leads to the unpredictable. But the heart is happiest when we follow essence, even when our logical minds tremble with fear.

Amid so many possibilities, 32 chooses the heart's knowledge instead of fear; chooses its wishes rather than its cravings. 32 gives form to the stress of life.

**33** Gradually, powerlessness ends. By following our hearts and making real choices, we gain access to a powerfulness that is greater than anything we have known up until now. Vitality and self-confidence are the outcome.

We now understand that self-confidence is the result of the effort the personality makes to tune itself to the essence. Self-confidence is not a character trait; it is the outcome of our willingness to dedicate our whole character to the achievement of a greater goal.

Although 33 is now used to being called Mr. or Ms. and being treated with respect, it is only now that childhood is really over. You are no longer the child of your parents. You are not the product of your environment. You think and feel, and yet you are more than your thoughts and feelings. You are self-made, powerful, and influential.

## 34

So much has happened. It is striking that the process has been extremely personal, painfully so in fact, but the end result is something that is not personal—it is the work that one does in the world. Everything is now translated into what you do and the influence you have through what you do.

34 is goal oriented.

As always, at the end of a seven-year cycle, we breathe a sigh of relief that the storm is over and that we have survived. Along with this comes a certain gnawing feeling that something new is on its way. In this case, the new doesn't bring crisis.

A basis has been formed. This can be built upon and specialization can be developed. The spiritual principle can become more visible in the setting of our daily lives.

## THE SIXTH PHASE
## 35 TO 42 YEARS
## CRYSTALLIZATION

This phase offers us the opportunity to join heart, head, *and* hands—feelings, thoughts, *and* deeds. Feelings and thinking can now be in agreement. Our deeds can now reflect how we *really* feel about things. The alternative is moral corruption.

The fullness of form is achieved. Everything learned and experienced to date crystallizes into a definite product, which is then offered with the greatest possible confidence to the community. The continuity of the community is served by our offering.

At the crossroads of continuity (which is highly valued by society) and discontinuity (which is essential for the individual), the midlife crisis develops.

*35 to 42 Crystallization*

**35** Johann Faust was 35 when he made his infamous pact with the evil genius Mephistopheles. The outcome of the pact was to choose the path of heartless intellect—thinking devoid of love. As a result of the pact, Faust lost his beloved, Gretchen.

At 35, we have to make a choice between the evil and the good genius. We can choose for further and further separation of head and heart, or we can choose for an ongoing convergence of the two.

The evil genius promises endless possibility; the good genius demands limitation. No wonder we so easily mistake the one for the other. The personality now gets the chance to learn and integrate the lesson of the theme we first encountered at the beginning of puberty, at 12: "In knowing how to lose, you will find."

The seven-year cycle that begins at 35 offers the opportunity to connect not only head and heart, but also hands; to connect feelings, thoughts, *and* actions. If we do this, not only will thoughts agree with feelings, but *actions* will also follow thoughts and feelings. This integration can only happen if the personality—the owner of head, heart, and hands—is willing to listen to the good genius.

The good and the evil genius aren't simply inner voices. We all know at least one evil or good genius in our immediate environment, so the choice faces us in both the inner and outer worlds.

35 wants to know more than the personality alone can grasp. It is therefore very important to choose our advisers and helpers carefully. The only real measure we have is love. Are we being offered a choice that brings us connection or separation? Will it bring greater unity or more fragmentation?

# 36

36 is a crossing of many ways. Receptivity and activity either conjoin or degenerate into hyperactivity or powerless passivity. Creativity is one choice; increasing tension and stress is the other. In this year, the consequences of personal idiosyncrasies are felt. You realize that life is based on certain unbreakable rules. There are limits to what one can permit oneself to do in one's personal life—life has rules that are more important than personal pleasure.

This means that 36 learns to see the value of discipline.

Discipline is not so much a moral attitude (although 36 may fall into that trap) as it is the realistic understanding that nothing is free. If you want to become an astronaut, you will have to quit smoking—it's as simple as that. If you want to live a life of love, if you want to devote yourself with heart and soul to your work, you may have to rein in some aspects of your personality.

36 calls us to deny what wasn't really ours in the first place. In so doing, we find our direction.

**37**   37 builds a new world. We say, "This is my home," and we put our whole being into it. We feel that we are supported by principles we don't fully understand yet, but which give us a feeling of trust.

*Trust* is our key word. In the general sense, it is trust in the Original Source that feeds all things. In particular, it is trust in our own powers and the knowledge that every stumbling stone is actually a stepping stone to something better. Vitality reaches a high point, and in this vital trust, we make our contribution to the world.

However, if we lose that trust, if we no longer use our willpower to energize our trust, we will become dull and depressed. The Source becomes cloudy, apathy leads to despair, the project stagnates. Only when we understand that despair is really an inner goad, do we make a start on clearing up the debris, cleaning out the well. At 37 we just makes the start; the rest will follow naturally.

Help is at hand, with one condition—we must open the door ourselves.

**38**

The easiest way is the right way!
How difficult it is to find the easiest
way.

The building project continues.
The social form crystallizes further.
Personal development and
fulfillment through work go hand
in hand.
    This is a period of fruitfulness.
Active steps are taken. Contradictory
elements are either integrated into
the whole or done away with totally.

This period asks for courage *and*
modesty. It requires taking steps
courageously and sacrificing with
modesty those things that don't
serve the "great plan" of progress.

38 purifies life so that life can be
receptive to what is coming.

## 39

39 is like that good dream, which, although slipping out of your mind soon after waking, nevertheless adds a certain glow to the rest of the day.

39 is an intangible, illusive vision, something that is just about to burst open, an intuitive realization that can't yet be rhymed with everyday experience.

Your daily work takes on an ever clearer form. You are busy with your career, concentrating to the maximum on the visible, perceivable reality.

Just at this moment a new keynote enters your life. It is like a sound heard only by the inner ear (the outer ear still focuses on the familiar outer world). There is possibly a feeling of conflict, a feeling of being torn, that you can't quite put your finger on.

It is worthwhile now to take some time out from the daily momentum on a regular basis to focus on what it is that you really want. See this as a form of meditation. By meditating in this way, you can make contact once more with the fine vibration of this new tone. What is important is that recognition leads to a conscious tuning and the beginning of a lasting relationship between the inner and outer ears.

In this year, in which wish and reality can easily come into conflict, a seed is planted that will need seven or eight years to grow and come to fruition.

**40**

At 40, we reach completed form. Everything we have learned and experienced up until now comes together into a finished product. This product is offered to the community in full confidence at 40. In so doing, 40 serves the continuity of the community.

There is also a shadow side to this. A law of life says that everything that wants to stay itself will run into problems.

At the crossroads of the continuity that is valued by the community and the discontinuity that is so valuable for the individual, the midlife crisis begins.

The individual sees that 40 represents the full measure of personal dignity.

In other words, 40 is the number in which the ego's resistance to life is expressed to its fullest extent.

The new keynote that was experienced as a promise at 39 is often experienced as a threat at 40—what is heard by the inner ear is ignored. If that happens, life becomes desolate and meaningless. Nothing is experienced as a fulfillment anymore. On the surface, you carry on with all sorts of interests and projects; deep inside, you know that life has become lifeless. You become cynical, blasé.

40 puts things to the test. Will you carry on investing in illusion, or will you look at last at the reality of your own life?

In your journey through the desert of life, you will become either an insatiable hunter of stimulation or a seer of reality who returns to yourself.

*35 to 42 Crystallization*

# 41

41 is the year of the lightning flash—revelatory and shocking.

The great hurdle of 40 has been passed. At 41, you see a light. Not a small light, but a light. After the light, darkness again.

In this light, your own personal resistance to life is revealed to you—the defense mechanisms of your personality. These mechanisms are also recognized by the outside world as fossilized structures, your defenses against life. At the same time, you experience a force that is greater than all defenses—pure light.

The realization dawns: Nobody has ever done me wrong and nobody can ever do me right! This is *my* existence—I can choose light or I can choose darkness. I can look back in anger or I can create a new reality.

## THE SEVENTH PHASE
## 42 TO 49 YEARS
## THROUGH THE
## LABYRINTH

In the seventh phase, life's autumn begins. You have passed the halfway mark, and you know it.

There's nothing you can do that you haven't already done, and everything you have done before has left its mark. You are surrounded by self-created forms and structures that have begun to lead their own lives. These creations now form a labyrinth, through which you try to find a way.

Gradually, you begin to see the relativity of things, but how to deal with unfulfillment remains a central question.

This is a period of purification. If you dare to find your way in the dark to the heart of the labyrinth and meet yourself there, including the selves that you *don't* want to be, fear falls away. You begin to realize that forms, structures, and relationships might actually be expressions of life itself.

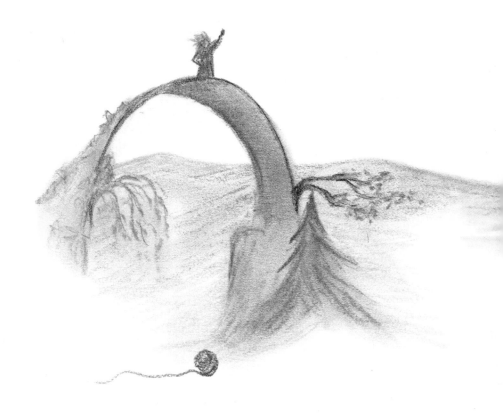

*42 to 49 Through the Labyrinth*

# 42

42 is half of life.

You have done it all already, and it shows! 42 is surrounded by self-created forms that have begun to lead lives of their own. You may or may not have a partner, friends, children, work. You have developed a certain relationship with your family; you are regarded in a specific way by the people around you; you have gathered possessions, experiences, knowledge; you live in a certain house; you have a certain body that looks different from all other bodies. All of these factors form a labyrinth through which you are trying to find your way.

At this time, the walls of the labyrinth may grow closer and closer, so that life seems to become a prison. You may see a way out—a light that you run toward. Whatever happens, the lesson in this phase of life is that *real* freedom comes when you consider not only what you have done, but also what you have left undone.

The questions now are these: What have you avoided until now? What could you have become that you haven't become? Why? Which reality have you been fleeing?

The forms of existence petrify into a labyrinth, but everything you have been avoiding also gathers together, in the depths of that exis-tence, into a dark shape—the shadow of yourself. This shadow lives at the center of the labyrinth.

If we can develop the desire to face everything we have been avoiding and find our own answers, we will awaken out of the past. At that moment, the labyrinth will become a path of light.

42 will then be the year of new adulthood. The old is finished and becomes the raw material for the new.

**43** When we get to know ourselves in the utmost detail, we come to a disconcerting conclusion: there is better company imaginable! This is a formidable blow to the self-respect of those of us who always wanted to be the most entertaining, the most friendly, the most attractive.

It begins with the realization that you are really getting older. Processes are irreversible. The lines in your face are getting deeper, and if you're not careful, your habits will also become ingrained before you realize what is happening. The things that weren't resolved when we were young and flexible certainly won't dissolve now of their own accord. 43 is chained to an inflexible *doppelganger*—a double of yourself. The bondage is both internal and external. Friends and lovers also suddenly seem to have extremely unpleasant character traits. Their dark sides show through everything. "This isn't what I want!" you cry defiantly, in a vain attempt to bend destiny and change the other. But fate doesn't allow itself to be changed by sheer force of will.

The other is really another—you can't change her!

The only one who has to bend is you.

If you bend, in acceptance of reality, reality-as-fate will melt before your eyes. You will stop being the narcissistic center of your own small, self-created world.

If you can offer yourself to life, with everything you have, then the fetters will fall away and you will find that you have a place in a greater creation.

**44**   As our feelings of bondage weaken, along with our obsession with the unfinished and imperfect, a new source of energy emerges. What has been a hindrance suddenly becomes a help. When what was felt to be unacceptable is now accepted, when we no longer allow ourselves to adopt an "attitude" because life isn't how we wanted it to be, we find that we have tapped into an enormous well of energy.

The self-reflective quality of your personality may continue, and you may still measure yourself by past criteria, but again and again the mirror of self-reflection breaks and you are surprised by the power of your new life energy and the naturalness and depth with which real knowledge comes through when needed.

There is one other possibility: that you keep self-reflection alive at all costs. If you choose that way, then self-reflection freezes into a self-satisfied smile. This person becomes dispassionate and unreachable. Life is over.

**45** As you let yourself be guided by your new source of strength, you will find that you are less and less dependent on strong characters around you. You see yourself reflected less and less in the examples of others, and you believe less and less that there is one way and one way only to live life.

Every house has its share of troubles, and every mind has its dark corners. There are no generally appropriate ways of dealing with those troubles and dark corners. The pat answers may serve their function for a time, like the womb that served its purpose for a time. But at some point, you have to leave the womb behind.

There is no answer to be found outside of yourself. You *are* the answer, the only answer to the question that your life poses.

Amazingly, this realization doesn't lead to a feeling of isolation. Yes, you may feel alone more often, even helpless in the beginning. But you will become *less* lonely and isolated.

And because you are becoming incomparable with others, you occupy your own place in the world more and more. You have something worth saying, you know how to say it, and people *hear* you.

**46** The forms that life presents us, the structures and relationships, are not only a defense against life, but also an expression of it. Forms are frozen music. Existence-as-labyrinth is like a majestic structure, built according to divine proportions, measurements, and numbers. The shadow, no longer rejected, becomes a source of power. This energetic dark side of human consciousness is the key to connecting with the great rhythm of life that vibrates throughout the universe.

At this time, it goes without saying that we must leave behind us those people who aren't tuned in to the rhythm of life. The real point now is no longer whether you find someone sympathetic or unsympathetic, but whether they are tuned in to the same ground tone. You form relationships with people who are "tuned in" the same way that you are. These relationships lead to new creative developments.

The ground tone that started at 39 has now become a melody that accompanies you through the rest of your life. By learning and by following this melody, the obstacles encountered earlier in life will be transformed, and you will find that you have become an instrument in the hands of life.

*42 to 49 Through the Labyrinth*

**47** How to deal with unfulfillment remains one of the key questions in this period of life.

We have grown milder toward life, however, and we begin to realize that no other person, or in a larger sense life itself, can make up for this lack of fulfillment we feel. What counts is not the elimination of our frustration, but rather the willingness to be fruitful, no matter what the circumstances.

Frustration, the longing for the impossible, the preoccupation with fate, and the sense of being tied down are not phenomena in isolation and they certainly are not justifications for acting up or adopting an attitude. They are just manifestations of the tenaciousness of the personality that always wants to have its own way, turning the impossible into a problem to be solved.

If, on the other hand, the personality can accept incompletion as a fact, then the impossible can become the starting point for some quiet observation. It is this opportunity of the impossible that 47 brings. 47 can be a year of perceiving truth without passing judgment. From now on, we aren't looking for results in the first place. Rather, we do things for their own sake.

**48** Society has a great need for the fruits of quiet reflection. At 48, you can personally experience how sought after the natural wisdom that you have gained in the last few years is. As a mature person, you are valued, especially by those who struggle with the limitations of the material world, but who are still ruled by their own conservatism. They ask for advice, turning to the wise judge that 48 has become for yourself and others.

The *really* wise judge knows the tension between creativity and law, rhythm and meter.

Categorical answers are foreign to you, both in your own life and elsewhere.

Growth is stimulated from what we have experienced.

## THE EIGHTH PHASE
## 49 TO 56 YEARS
## GUIDING AND BEING
## GUIDED

You guide and are guided. You have made it through the labyrinth, thanks to the thread of love that was continually placed in your hands. Realizing this, you are thankful and gain the right to guide others.

The power of the outer world begins to wane; the inner world emerges more and more. If you shut yourself off from this inner world, you have only two possibilities: You resist the passage of time and try desperately to hold on to youth, or you succumb to the power of time, your energies extinguished.

You take stock of your life. What have you really achieved? What can you be proud of? Were you nothing more than a replaceable cog in a giant machine?

The game of trying to outshine others is over. We won or we lost. In any case, if we are still trying to play the game, then we certainly have lost.

**49** The symbol for 49 is the candle: a simple uprising form bearing light, feeding the light with its own being.

It may sometimes seem as though individuality (and the earlier stage of the individual, the ego) can develop only if we can distinguish ourselves from others and become independent. However, if love is missing, then independence is impossible. Without love, the drive for independence leads only to fragmentation.

49 realizes and experiences that all becoming, all growth from early youth until this time, takes place in an atmosphere of care and protection. The Great Mother has always protected us, even during our loneliest moments when we thought we had truly been deserted by God and all humanity.

It often feels as if the Great Mother deliberately causes us pain, as if, as the legend of the Greek mother-goddess Demeter tells us, she lays us in a great fire. Sooner or later, the realization dawns that this fire is a healing fire. It doesn't lead to our death or to endless suffering, but to liberation from all that is *not really us*. That is reason enough to be thankful.

For 49, thankfulness becomes a reality. If we were to sin against this reality, for instance by denying it, we would become the isolated, helpless children that have always lived inside us as possibilities.

For seven years, we have been putting all of our efforts into finding the way through the labyrinth of our lives. This process has purified us, maybe even transformed us. A greater unity has emerged between our thinking and our feeling, our head and our heart.

*49 to 56 Guiding and Being Guided*

We now know the following: that we made it through thanks to the thread of love, continually placed in our hands. We thought that it was our own doing. In fact, we were being guided.

In our thankfulness, we begin to guide others.

**50** The guidance we can give is this: in this world of time, we aim for the timeless.

The questions and problems we are presented with need to be analyzed as precisely as possible. We must look for causes and analyze possible effects.

While we are busy examining and analyzing, we are also aware that we don't know the *real* cause and we can never know the *real* effect. Past and future are projections of our own.

The wonder is that life keeps manifesting, despite and even thanks to our projections.

*49 to 56 Guiding and Being Guided*

The future, whatever we want to make of it, is something that comes to us. It is a gift.

Although rooted in material existence, 50 is oriented toward the essence that wants to manifest fully in everything.

Those of us who regard temporal happenings with both eyes open, while keeping the one inner eye focused on the timeless, are like biblical patriarchs, leading people through the desert from oasis to oasis. Maybe that is why, in Holland, they say that 50 has "seen Abraham."

**51** 51 is the year of the well. The *I Ching* says, "You can move the city, but you cannot move the well." You can change the nature and form of existence, but you have no influence over the power that animates you.

In this period, you realize how little you can actually achieve through the exercise of power, and yet how influential you really are. For instance, you are aware of a certain direction that is right for yourself and possibly for others. It is crucial that you don't use force in following this path, because force will change the very nature of the path.

The direction you take may not lead directly to the goal you had in mind. Rather, when you move in that direction, you will become privy to information that points you in another direction. If you then follow the first path to the bitter end, life will become joyless and you will not reach your goal. Only by listening carefully while walking the path do you find the direction that is really worth following, the path that comes out best in the end.

This is the difference between fundamentalism and free development, between the old government and a new society.

**52** In youth, every person has promise. Many have great promise. Great promise may appear to be a blessing, but it is often more of a curse. The person with promise and those around him or her easily get caught up in the enchantment of many possibilities. They fantasize over possibilities, forgetting that a promise can become reality only if choices and sacrifices are made.

It is a great temptation for those with promise to keep all options open, so as not to limit themselves. If they succumb to this temptation, the real potential can become hidden like a rare plant in an overgrown garden. While the garden may look very luxuriant, the rare plant will not come to fruition. The garden must be pruned if the real possibility is to come through. Pruning is a painful process.

Life cuts and hacks at us. We lose people who were dear to us; what we thought we had is taken away. We become disillusioned. We lose the very things that we thought were essential to fulfilling our promise.

The promise comes through at last. Autumn has now truly set in. Fruit hangs on the branches.

# 53

53 sits by the window, looking out and observing the transitoriness of youth.

In the afternoon light, life has great beauty. Sharp lines soften. We see that all things are part of a greater whole. In the darkening of the light, we also see that the visible forms of things are temporary.

Sitting by the window, we know that dusk is approaching, that it will soon be dark. Soon, the children playing just across the street will not be distinguishable against the background.

All things return to their point of origin. All temporal existence comes to an end. 53 knows that, but also that the *quality* of perception is not determined by the outer, but by the inner light. If we don't realize that we know that, we have only two possibilities: to resist the passage of time in a desperate attempt to stay young, or to succumb to the power of time and become a burned-out fire. In both cases, time takes irrevocable possession of us. Night comes, and even our contours disappear. We dissolve into nothing—with a struggle or with resignation.

As the strength of the outer world wanes, the inner world can break open. In the failing outer light, facing toward the inner world, 53 guides the way.

**54** The motives that once drove us count less. Existence can now be valued for its own sake. It is either nice to be alive or it isn't. Whatever the future may hold can't change this present moment one iota. Whatever we do for another, if we don't do it willingly, it isn't going to benefit anyone at all. The quality of existence is determined by our state of mind, our vision, our effort.

The big question now is, What have *I really* done with my life? What can I be proud of? Was I no more than a small replaceable cog in an enormous machine?

It is vitally important for 54 not to be crippled by the feeling of melancholy that veils this question. It is a question that deserves a straightforward answer.

The funny thing is that when we take an honest look at our achievements, they turn out to be as transparent as the sky. Whatever we did, we brought nothing new under the sun.

The irony is that, when we accept this, an opening is created for the new to enter in. In a modest way, we can now make our unique contribution.

Simple as you are, you contribute your small stone to the communal structure.

## 55

The strength of individuality—the peculiarity of the individual—reaches its highest form at 55.

The second great cycle that began at 28 is coming to an end. Just as at 27, we are now approaching the point of departure, the point where life's journey began. In the first cycle (0–28 years) the cards of life were shuffled and dealt. We saw *what* we have in our hands. In this second cycle, the game was played out. We saw *how* we put what we have in our hands to use; we developed our own unique game style; we won or we lost. At 55, our game style reaches perfection.

At 55 we make our last move. The last move often determines the outcome of the game. This is a decisive year—there is still everything to play for.

*The Third Period*
*56 to 84*
*Spiritual Life*

## THE NINTH PHASE
## 56 TO 63 YEARS
## HEAVEN AND EARTH

It is sometimes painful to see that our grip on life fails. Time runs through our fingers like water. Everything passes so quickly. Yet at the same time there is that other pulse, deep within us—the steady heartbeat.

The temptation to forcefully adapt to that ever-changing world outside of our door resurfaces. If we give in to that temptation, we will be at best a poor copy of the others, eventually finding that we have painted ourselves into a corner. But if, rather than tuning in to the outer world, we tune in to our own inner sources, we will soon discover that we are actually centerpoints. As centerpoints, we offer not so much factual knowledge as insight. We are examples, pillars of strength.

A new alchemical process begins now. It gives us the chance to transform and to channel wisely the strength that has been burning away inside us since our youth. Those who know how to use this alchemy rejuvenate themselves. They transform vitality into fortitude and endurance.

## 56 Third Birth

This is the beginning of the third great twenty-eight-year cycle.

The first cycle is all about physical, emotional, and mental growth. The key word is *arising*. The birth at the beginning of existence is above all a physical birth, an incarnation. It is a physical miracle. At the first birth, the word becomes flesh.

The second cycle offers us the possibility to become unique and to make a contribution to the social world to which we belong. The key word is *shining*. The birth at the beginning of the second cycle is above all a mental birth. The personality begins to let its inner voice guide it in what it does. It connects the inner and outer worlds in a way that is uniquely its own, and in the process it discovers its own destiny. At the second birth, flesh learns to listen to the word.

The third cycle is about spiritualization and the return to the
Source. The relationships that were
built up during the second cycle
and the social structures that we
became part of begin to change or
break up, becoming transparent or
dissolving completely. The key
word is *declining*. The birth at the
beginning of the third cycle is
above all a spiritual birth—a birth
into the spirit. At the third birth,
the flesh becomes word.

There is a new interest in essential questions, in philosophy, and in
religion. Often, in the second cycle,
functionality was the central issue.
In the third cycle it is meaning in
the face of death. Life experience in
the second cycle ripens to wisdom
in the third.

56 finds new ways to balance
wishes and aspirations with the
expectations of others. If we refuse
to accept that the path we've been
following up until now can't be
continued linearly, we stagnate and
our environment stagnates with us.
If, on the other hand, we recognize
that letting go is needed to allow
reorientation to happen, we stay

supple and our new life's task will
be revealed to us. We will retain the
respect of our surroundings.

## 57

Increasing wisdom does not necessarily imply decreasing activity. However, your creative energy may be channeled into different activities; it may be less vital than before, and you may now accept the help of others more than you used to.

57 lets go a little. We command less; rather we share our vision. The influence we have and the help we offer are based on life experience. We recognize that personal development here is paired with a weakening of faculties there. We know that we can put our creative impulses to work only if we recognize that we too need some assistance.

This is possible for 57. In helping, we don't put ourselves on a pedestal; in accepting help, we don't feel degraded.

**58** Creativity can happen only within the boundaries of time and space. Oh, how you wish for other possibilities, other worlds! But life is about concrete reality. Therefore, it is sometimes painful to experience how your grasp on life weakens. Time runs through your fingers like water. Everything is going so fast! Yet, deep inside, there is that other tempo—the steady heartbeat.

The temptation is great to force yourself to adapt to the hasty world outside. But if you do that, you will only be a poor copy of the life of others and end up in situations from which you will have difficulty extricating yourself. It is like running for a train that is already moving away—however fast you run, you will not be able to catch it, and if you catch hold of the door and don't let go soon enough, an accident is unavoidable.

Being creatively busy now is possible only when you become the centerpoint. Let the questions come to you, and don't answer them in a habitual way. It is not factual knowledge that people are asking you for, but insight; not speed, but timing.

Insight and timing are gifts that you have to offer when you realize, and realize lastingly, that space and time don't ask anything of you. Rather, they are possibilities in which you move and express yourself.

This is the guiding thought of 58: Time doesn't make me hasty; space doesn't box me in. Whatever the circumstances, I share myself creatively.

**59**

*If I am that I am*
*then time*
*is like the opening and closing*
*of a multi-colored fan*
*that from birth until death,*
*I am.*

59 looks back at life. We see how
much we allowed our lives to be
determined by the impressions we
wanted to make on others and how
much we let ourselves be guided by
our deepest wishes and
knowledge. We see the
results of the
choices
we made.

Fear and love
have been our companions
through life. In the tension between
these two, our lives have taken on a
certain form.
    May this form now dissolve?

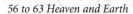

**60** Some Chinese Taoist schools believe that one can dedicate oneself to the very highest only when 60 approaches. The ancient Greeks called 60 the age of the philosopher. The philosopher is one who seeks the deepest meaning of things and fundamental values.

Philosophers begin with themselves. They observe their own relativity *and* immortality. They put things into their proper context without becoming cynical. They suggest theses without becoming dogmatic.

Self-knowledge is the first principle of the philosopher. We are gentle, but don't gloss over the bad. We distinguish, but don't judge. In this way, we separate the grain from the chaff. When we give advice, the truth seems obvious, so that questioners feel that they found the answer in themselves.

The philosopher's last word is silence.

## 61

Fire feeds itself with anything that is flammable. If it can find no more fuel, it smolders for a time and then dies.

In the middle of summer, a fool can start a forest fire—it only takes one match. It takes great skill to keep a winter fire burning night and day with little fuel. This is the skill that 61 starts to learn.

The vitality of youth can be unbridled. The wise person learns to be a keeper of the fire, to keep it together, to put it to use.

We no longer make ourselves dependent on outer fuel. We don't lose ourselves in passions and emotions. At the same time, we don't let the fire go out. We feed it with ourselves, because we have become fuel.

We are also the oven that encloses, controls, and directs the fire. We turn the small into the great, transforming vitality of spiritual power.

61 looks back at the lesser and greater fires in life—the loves, passions, outbursts; the enterprises taken on with enthusiasm. We look at how we used our fire, what we took on, and what we avoided.

Were we consumed by the fire, used up? Did we reject the fire and become cold and hard? Did we develop a respectful, mutual relationship with the fire?

An alchemical process begins at 61. It offers the possibility to wisely transform and direct the fuel that has been burning in us since our early youth. Those who practice this alchemy are rejuvenated. We become immortals, to borrow a term from the Chinese culture, which seems to have so much more eye for the possibilities of age than does Western culture.

You are immortal.

You are young and yet old; rich in experience, yet no experience limits you. At your journey's end, wherever you find yourself is your home.

You feed the genuine; the false you pass tirelessly by.

# 62

62 returns to roots. We contemplate our origins. We remember our parents, as if we were *their* parents. We remember the way they searched, became entangled, found. We break the last vestiges of emotional dependence that still connect us to them.

If you can regard your father and your mother in this way, no longer bound by a positive or negative image of them, you honor them as they are. You give them back to themselves. This is a form of forgiveness.

Remarkably, it is only by doing this that you gain access to the roots of your tree of life. You become a tribal chief!

As a chief, you know the power that governs your family, your tribe. You see the potential and the typical problems of this family, generation after generation, and you see how you have been busy your whole life trying to find your own personal answer to these tribal problems.

By honoring your father and mother as they are, you also disconnect them from that very power that led to your personal existence—the sexual power. This is very important, because your relationship to your father and mother, and their relationship to each other, to a large extent determines the development of your own sexual habits, patterns, and hang-ups. By letting go of your parents, you also let go of this network of sexual automatism.

In practice, this means that 62 looks back over life as a "mental ruminant." You let everything that you have experienced come to the surface again, experience it, digest it again. You digest your experiences so that you can review them from beginning to end and so that you can forgive the others and especially yourself.

At 62, we can find a new and freer relationship to our desires and, in so doing, we can heal the rift between the sexes. As tribal chiefs, we can help others find their own answer to the primal forces they are subject to.

## THE TENTH PHASE
## 63 TO 70 YEARS
## TOWARD SIMPLICITY

The tenth phase marks the beginning of life's winter. The appearance of things becomes less and less important. We enjoy life as it is.

In this phase, it becomes clear how much we have *lived* in the work we did. Did we do it because we had no choice—just to earn a living—or was our work something that came from inside? If the answer is the latter, we will find that the fire of life hasn't burned us to ashes or fossilized. Rather, it has burnished us into gold. We have tapped the inner ore.

Has a portway opened from the material to the immaterial world? Then there will be no ossification. Our experience will provide us with wise answers to everyday questions. Our greatest effectiveness will be in our simplicity.

**63** 63 was the last square in the "goose-board," where the path through life is represented by a spiral. The first to reach 63 wins and gets the "pot."

On your way to 63, you may have found yourself in the well (31), lost in the labyrinth (42), or experiencing a spell in prison (52). You overcame these obstacles on your own or with the help of others. At 58, you became aware of death as an unavoidable last station, without letting your life be ruled by this awareness. You have developed your own way of looking at things; you have found your own rhythm; you are now free to enjoy everything you have done during the game of life.

61 and 62 freed the inner fire. 63 enjoys life as it is, free and straight-forward.

63 is unique—an example that others can't follow, but can be stimulated by.

The tension is past. Head and heart no longer need to be kept apart, even for the sake of appearances. You can be objectively subjective, subjectively objective. You can think as you feel and feel as you think.

When the tensions are released, the consequences of tension dissolve. But before they dissolve, they appear on the surface. Feelings of sympathy and antipathy are reviewed in the light of the head-heart choice. Especially in your relationships with your children and grandchildren, and with others from younger generations, you realize how much you have been influenced by your own duality.

The part of yourself that you valued less was either rejected further or overvalued as a form of compensation.

You realize that you have favored some above others because of your own idiosyncrasies.

Relationships undergo realignments. As much as you want to know and love yourself fully, you also want to love and know your children and grandchildren.

You honor your children as they are; you are a parent who deserves to be honored.

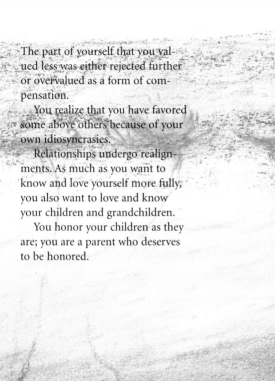

**65**  Ashes, fossil, nugget of gold. That is 65.

65 has been ground to ashes by the machine that is the world; or has become stubbornly immovable, paralyzing any surrounding actions; or has transformed life experiences to living wisdom.

We may have burned out or become a fossil, but fortunately it is also possible that we may still be sprightly as a result of the work we have done. In that case, we have a mass of experience, and we are wise. In the fire of daily existence, we have not turned into ashes or stone, but into gold. The "inner ore" has been released.

That which is but ash shall return to ash. If we allow an opening in our physical existence to give access to the spiritual world, then no overpowering fossilization will have set in. In that case, 65 has an individual answer, based upon mature experience, to the questions of everyday life.

This answer refers to a new possibility of life, which is not seen by one's physical awareness. 65 gives long-term vision.

## 66

66 says: "The law of life that I obey is the same as the power that animates me. I gain nothing anymore from my worldly achievements. I no longer adhere to worldly regulations. It is not important who I am, how you see me, how you think I should be. I am, in love. Everything else is in order."

66 has no pretensions. You fit into existing forms. It is precisely in the unemphatic that you find you are most useful.

# 67

67 sees the potential of growth and development in all things. You see that growth needs darkness as much as it needs light, that need can be just as character forming as luxury. In your world, good and bad are no longer two independent entities.

67 knows that everything that happens is helpful. Objects, events, and circumstances aren't things, they are medicines, bitter and sweet, that begin to do their work only when the patient—the suffering, searching human being—takes them. When everything life offers is taken, when the medicine is taken as it is, the patient will heal.

67 works quietly. You organize; you set things in their place—this a little more in the light, that a little more in the shadow. Minimum influence results in maximum effect.

**68** The key word for 68 is *defenseless-ness.*

People think that defenselessness is weakness, but that isn't so. Defenselessness is possibly the greatest strength we can employ for the benefit of something that goes beyond self-preservation. The small defends itself with fighting spirit; the great is served by defenseless-ness. Defenselessness presupposes trust. However, if 68 opens up receptively, it is possible to act by not acting. This nonaction has nothing to do with laziness. It is being present as totally as possible, without fears, without prejudices or expectations. If you are so at rest, then you actually are moved in the opposite direction. It is one possibility. It is what 68 is, not something else. This is what is meant by nondoing.

That is 68—busy in matter, following the lines of light.

**69** The living word breaks through all defenses. The ear cannot block out the truth. But we, having heard the truth, can turn away, push away what was heard, change it, forget it. We can then be furious at the messenger of truth and try to project all our disgruntlement at this person. This doesn't change the fact that truth has been heard—for just one moment.

69 has the potential to see and to express truth in the simplest of terms. If you are wise, you won't throw pearls before swine or feed roses to asses. You give your gift— the living word—to those who will open their inner ear to it.

69 is quiet, amid all social contacts. Speech is silver, hearing gold, silence the philosopher's stone.

## THE ELEVENTH PHASE
## 70 TO 77 YEARS
## THROUGH DEATH

It is an ancient image: Everything that happens is enclosed by the "ouroboros," the tail-eater, the snake that bites its own tail. It marks the boundaries of all things.

This snake is the symbol of time and the laws of time to which all things are subjected. One of the most important laws, if not *the* most important, is that everything that is created must one day be destroyed. Everything that is born also dies. In other words, living in time is dying.

In some images of the ouroboros, you can see that it doesn't exist of itself; it is "let down" out of another reality that is invisible to our eyes.

This expresses the fact that the temporal world is not the ultimate reality and that death at the end of temporal reality is not a definitive end.

Death is a watcher. Death is, according to the holy books, the last opponent. Beyond it lies another reality. We cannot express what this reality will look like in the language of space and time. But the reality beyond death *is* knowable, because death is not only our last opponent, it is also our opponent *within* life.

From moment to moment, we can let ourselves be ruled by our fear, which in the final analysis is always the fear of death. We can shy away from the so-called little deaths of every day and struggle to stay as we were, whatever the cost, to keep what we had.

Doing this, we resist the impulses of life—the hand that lets down the snake—and take no more risks. The paradox is that you can only escape death in death. Fleeing what we could call living death—death that breaks into the continuity of life and so opens us up to new life—we become lifeless. We become rigid, lose our thirst for life, become fixated on everything that can go wrong. We become a living dead. There is nothing anyone can do from the outside to help such a person. Unless we—from inside—turn ourselves around and, despite our fears and worries, repent to life, we remain

dead. It is this living death that Jesus referred to when he said; "Let the dead bury the dead."

In the years from 70 to 77, we are forcefully offered the opportunity to recognize and approach death as our lifelong companion. Where we were dead so as to avoid life, now we can let life in. This phase offers us the most essential opportunity of a second chance. In all things, the ultimate question is put forth; the answer will be ultimately redeeming.

Inherent to this second chance is the fact that you are freed from illusion, even from the strongest of all illusions—that you can somehow survive by projecting yourself forward in time, whether through your children, your work, your creations, your influence. Free of illusions, there is nothing in the temporal world that can trap you, and death as a metaphor of finality no

longer affects you. "Then you die," as the German mystic Jakob Böhme put it, "before you die." On the other hand, if death catches you while you are trying to escape, you will "decay into death."

The years 70 to 77 are years of exhaustion, resignation, or acceptance, and all points in between. You resign yourself to defeat, or you are grateful, or you have accomplished what you set out to accomplish. Letting go, you are taken up. The end of the road is in sight. Going is peace.

## THE TWELFTH PHASE
## 77 TO 84
## ETERNAL LIFE

If there is no death at the frontier of life, then life is just what it is. The world offers no promise, poses no danger. There is no future to bring what isn't already there, no other to make things better or worse. Time has become eternity, life eternal life. There is peace, and nothing can persist in the face of this peace. All experience is wave-like—rising out of, manifesting, returning to. Nothing remains standing in time. Joy you can't hold, suffering you can't repress. Joy becomes suffering, suffering joy; they are manifestations of life, as waves are manifestations of water.

All of the potentialities of this one life flow out into this one place: this place where I now am. Nothing is impossible, because nothing beyond myself is wished. Time translates who I am in ebb and flow. Nothing is waiting in the wings. I am time. Here I am in eternity.

No longer a participant, I am an observer, observing my creation. No longer a victim, but a creator, my creation is my act of love. No longer possessed, but being a lover, my act of love is continual recognition.

I am old and tired, tired of years. I am young, full of amazement. I am the beginning, and the end, and everything in between. The hand that enfolds me in love is myself, in thankfulness. I am.

# GENERAL COMMENTARY

Numbers can be arranged according to many systems (for instance, the prime numbers, as I mentioned in the personal commentary). With almost every number you can choose, these systems overlap each other. In describing each individual year, I have constantly attuned myself to the fabric that these systems create as they cross and recross. Much could be said about these different systems and the ways in which they come together, but most of that doesn't belong in this book—after all, this is not a book about numbers. I have confined myself in the following commentary to a description of the rhythms for the numbers one, three, and four, which are all directly related to the twelve phases of seven years that are the focus of this book.

## ONE AND ONE

The basic rhythm is undoubtedly one. It is the rhythm of unity underlying everything, embracing everything, and expressing everything. Each and every number is a manifestation of the unity of one.

The rhythm of one is our first multiplication table. One is the beginning. Add one, and one becomes two. Repeat ad infinitum.

Three, four, five, a hundred, a thousand, a million . . . again and again one is added to what already exists. This is how numbers come into being and how, according to myth, everything comes into being.

Historically, everything emerges from unity, the primordial beginning, and everything is re-created out of that unity every single moment. There seems to be a line of ongoing casualty through time, in which the twos, the threes, and the fours, and all the numbers start leading their own lives once created. Everything is constantly being given a new chance.

Life as a whole is *one*—birth and death are part of it. This unity presents us—as I wrote in the preface—with a gift, year after year, that suits our age, that we can unwrap and accept in our lives. This gift is the impulse, the inspiration that comes from the unity—a continually renewed expression of life. We have the right to accept this gift or to reject it if, for instance, we think it is too dangerous. Yes, new possibilities always hold risks. We can't use them without getting involved. To be able to accept something new in our lives, we often have to give up something old and familiar. This causes pain, worry, unease.

This is also why people so often prefer to reject a new reality in favor of keeping an old and familiar one. Avoidance of change seems to be the easiest way, and yet it does not solve the problem, for one has to pay a price even for the gift that is rejected: the impulse or inspiration, once excluded, becomes distorted and demonical in nature. That which is left undone will turn itself against us and burden our lives with all of the troubles we think of as destiny or fate. In describing the individual years, I regularly point out how the rejected gift can become deformed and what fate this brings about.

Luckily for us, this fate that we bring over ourselves is not a definitive fate. It continues only as long as we continue refusing to accept life's birthday gifts. Every moment, the opportunity for recovery is present, and in the great rhythm of life there are even various phases that are particularly designed with recovery in mind. For instance, in the phase of life around forty—the so-called midlife crisis—those issues that were left unresolved during puberty resurface and can be solved.

This brings us to the most important theme of the life phases. But before we can go delve into this, we must first acquaint ourselves with the rhythms of three and four—the fundamental elements of the life phases.

## THREE TIMES TWENTY-EIGHT

The great rhythm of three is also called the law of *rising, shining, and declining*. This is a well-known law. We see it everywhere around us. Everything that comes into being in time is subjected to time—from roses to birds to human beings to planets to stars. It applies to life on a small scale and on a large scale. On the small scale, every moment—just as each thought, each contact—has a starting point at which it seems to appear out of nowhere, a middle part at which it develops to the full, and an end point at which it comes to an end. On the large scale, this rhythm vibrates through the whole of existence, from birth to death. Everything that is born knows growth. It shines for a few moments or ages, and then it perishes.

The first third of the archetypal time span of eighty-four years, the first twenty-eight years, is in the *rising period*, the second third is in the *shining period*, and the last third is in the *declining period*.

In the first of these three phases there is growth, growth, and more growth. Human beings experience a tremendous physical growth, from baby to adult. We develop on an emotional level; our sympathies and antipathies crystallize; and we experience a tremendous mental development.

Moreover, we learn in the first twenty-eight years of life what it means to stand on our own feet and to be connected to our environments; we become people and we become social beings. In summary, the first twenty-eight years is a period of *building the personality*.

At the end of this period there is a choice: Do you choose to become an independent individual who finds your own way in life and adds your own creative contribution, or do you choose at all costs to remain part of a certain group to which you "belong"?

If you choose the second option, you can play a social role in an excellent way as a developed person, and you can really *shine* in a particular function or position. Outwardly, you can do quite well in the coming life phase, but deep down inside, something is lacking. The person who is afraid of unpopularity will remain a child in his or her environment and will never become an individual.

If you go for the first option, the coming phase will be characterized by a reorientation, possibly leading to a transformation of the personality developed in the first twenty-eight years. The personality can now become an individual that fulfills a unique destiny as a creative being. Thus, this second period is the time of *becoming an individual*. For everyone, the period from twenty-eight to fifty-six is a time of great productivity. In these twenty-eight years, our lives take on a certain shape—we get jobs, positions, circles of friends; we may find partners, have children, and gather possessions about us.

At the end of the second period —around fifty-six years—we come to the second great crossroads in life. The questions here are these: Can you acknowledge that the period of *shining* is over and that decline will set in? Can you see that this decline offers new possibilities in life? If you are looking only for eternal youth and want to remain forever active and productive, you cannot enter this new phase and you cannot harvest its fruits. You may be able to live for a while above your "vital means" and make believe that you do have eternal life; nevertheless, growth that is kept going artificially cannot go on indefinitely. At some point, there must be a collapse that will be much more drastic than a gradual transition toward decline.

If you enter the third period— from fifty-six to eighty-four or older—consciously, physical decline can open the way to spiritualization. You return to the Source and find renewed interest in the meaning of life. In the second period, goal orientation was your main focus; in the third period, it is about meaning in the face of death. This third period is the time of *spiritual life.*

The road of development from rising to shining to declining is a linear one. It starts with birth and ends with death. It is, as the Chinese would say, a yang road; it is all or nothing. You take your chance, you learn, you transform, or you are too late and you miss the boat. Over is over. It is all about manifesting or not manifesting. You live fully and consciously and become imperishable, or your life is lived for you by others and you become a missed chance.

## FOUR TIMES
## TWENTY-ONE

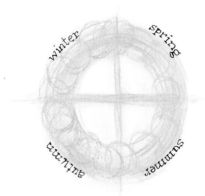

Alongside the linear development
of three there is division by four.
The rhythm of four is the cyclic
path of experience. Four is the
number that represents the eternal
relationship of the two great powers
of light and darkness. We can sum-
marize the four phases of light and
darkness in this way: light increases,
darkness is illuminated, darkness
increases, light is eclipsed. We find
these four phases everywhere in our
cyclic calendar. We discern four
"shifts" in the twenty-four-hour
day: morning (increasing light),
noon (the illumination of the darkness), evening (increasing darkness)
and night (the eclipsing of the
light); the lunar month has four
weeks that correspond to the four
phases of the moon; the solar year
is divided into the four seasons. In
all of these quaternary cycles, the
last phase always passes over into
the first. The cyclic road has no
definite end. Spring becomes summer, summer becomes autumn,
autumn becomes winter, and winter once more becomes spring. The
rhythm of four is clearly dis-
cernible in the life of the human
being. Up until our twenty-first
year, we are in the spring of our

lives; between twenty-one and forty-two—the summer of life—vitality reaches its peak; life's autumn begins around the forty-second year—vitality decreases, the harvest of life is ready to be brought in; winter starts around the sixty-third year—a period of rest and turning inward. At the age of eighty-four (or at the time of death), the cycle has come to an end and a new life—a new cycle—is about to begin.

In the cycle of four, life constantly renews itself. There is great kindness here; nothing is lost forever; there is always a new chance. The earthy, supporting, mothering side of life expresses itself in the rhythm of four. It is, as the Chinese would say, a yin rhythm.

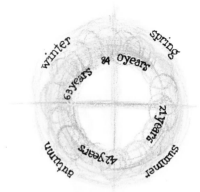

## THREE AND FOUR

Three is the number of Father Time, who says, in the words of an old Dutch New Year's Song, "Hours and days and months and years pass by like a shadow." Four is the number of Mother Time. She says, "After a storm comes a calm." Now it may seem that in the rhythm of life, these two exist independently of each other. In fact, the opposite is true—they belong together. They penetrate each other and they complement each other. This is just as well, because on their own, each of them is one-sided. The linear principle of rising, shining, and declining is too hard and too singular if it isn't complemented by the cyclic principle. The cycle of light and darkness merely repeats itself endlessly without the linear principle to give direction.

The primal pattern of life's rhythm points the way to wholeness. The linear principle and the cyclic principle are not opposed to each other, nor are they separate from each other: they are interwoven with each other. Each of the three periods of twenty-eight years is divided into four phases of seven years. That is how the cyclic expresses itself within the linear.

On the other hand, each of the four periods of twenty-one years is divided into three phases of seven years. That is how the linear expresses itself within the cyclic.

Within the total archetypal life span of eighty-four years, there are twelve phases of seven years. Twelve is the number of time and of life in time: our day has twelve hours, our solar year has twelve months, the zodiac has twelve signs. In twelve, cyclic and linear time come together.

In every life phase an aspect of the rhythm of three meets an aspect of the rhythm of four. New relationships are constantly forming. Life is an interweaving of male and female rhythms, yang and yin rhythms that begin at the same point—birth. During our lifetime, yin and yang separate. It is not until the very end of the last phase that they come together again, and the cycle is completed.

Each period of seven years can be seen as a phase on the way from unity through duality toward a new unity. It is just as much a phase on the linear road of development as on the cyclic road of experience. Each of the twelve phases of life can be described as the meeting of the yang road and the yin road in two sets of concepts (rising, shining, and declining; and spring, summer, autumn, and winter).

The key words of these concepts can be explained in a simple way. Let's take, for instance the key word associated with the sixth phase of life (from 35 to 42). This phase may bring some sadness because the "sunniest" time of life is almost over, but because of the fullness of existence and the wealth of colors and forms and discoveries, that sadness burns off almost as immediately as an autumn fog (Declining of Summer). We perform great feats, we are in the

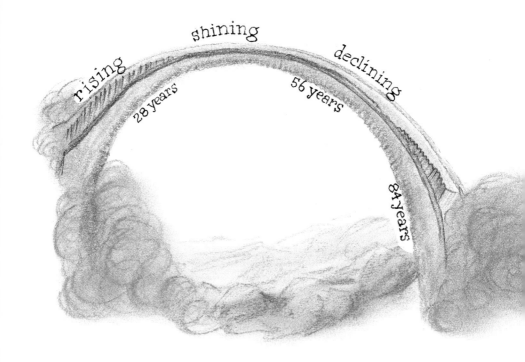

rising

shining

declining

28 years

56 years

84 years

prime of our lives; and we give shape to our individuality in a clear-cut form, in a creative rather than a reflective way (the Summer of Shining). At the end of this phase, around the fortieth year, self-reflection increases. The sadness of former days can lead to melancholy; we may constantly ask questions; and we may begin to doubt our certainties and goals as the seventh phase of life approaches (the Rising of Autumn and the Autumn of Shining).

Twelve sets of key words form the basis of the descriptions of the life phases with which each period of seven years is introduced in this book. I want to conclude this general commentary with the complete text of the twelve life phases:

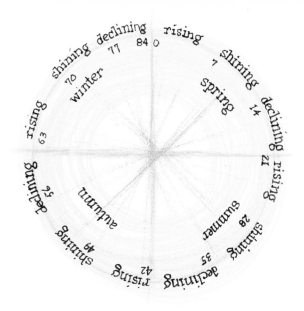

| | | | |
|---|---|---|---|
| 0–7 | the Spring of RISING<br>the Rising of SPRING | 42–49 | the Autumn of SHINING<br>the Rising of AUTUMN |
| 7–14 | the Summer of RISING<br>the Shining of SPRING | 49–56 | the Winter of SHINING<br>the Shining of AUTUMN |
| 14–21 | the Autumn of RISING<br>the Declining of SPRING | 56–63 | the Spring of DECLINING<br>the Declining of AUTUMN |
| 21–28 | the Winter of RISING<br>the Rising of SUMMER | 63–70 | the Summer of DECLINING<br>the Rising of WINTER |
| 28–35 | the Spring of SHINING<br>the Shining of SUMMER | 70–77 | the Autumn of DECLINING<br>the Shining of WINTER |
| 35–42 | the Summer of SHINING<br>the Declining of SUMMER | 77–84 | the Winter of DECLINING<br>the Declining of WINTER |

# THE FIRST PHASE
## 0 TO 7 YEARS
## COMING FROM HEAVEN

Here are the first shoots of human life. Coming from the unknown, the child arrives on Earth. Giving her a name, her parents call her *their* child, but in the beginning, she is more a child of the *oneness* of creation than of the world of duality. She doesn't yet recognize herself as *I*. She doesn't yet distinguish herself from her surroundings.

The child is completely dependent on his surroundings for his needs—food, warmth, love, and so on. Without the aid of his surroundings, he would soon die.

After a while, the first *I* awareness begins to develop. The child becomes shy, self-conscious; she begins to develop a certain character. No longer continually embedded in *unity*, the child leaves paradise.

In this time, the child has grown considerably. He has learned an enormous amount: he can walk and talk, he is toilet trained, and he has developed some practical skills. The child has an insatiable thirst for knowledge. In no other period of life does so much happen than in these first seven years.

The child is now ready to enter the world.

## THE SECOND PHASE
## 7 TO 14 YEARS
## ALL THIS THAT I AM

The child learns to know himself from all sides. He grows in all senses of the word, finds real friends (male and female), and belongs to a group or a club or a gang. He begins to develop a clear-cut personality.

By the end of this period, the child has really grown, but with growth comes the feeling that she is pushing against the limits of her world. She is still in contact, emotionally, with the place of *oneness* from which she originated, but she finds that space, time, and the discoveries she is continually making in this space-time demand virtually all her attention.

## THE THIRD PHASE
## 14 TO 21 YEARS
## THE WHEEL TURNS

In this phase, contradictions come to the fore. It is marked by inner struggle and struggle with our environment. The wheel of life turns; what was below is now above, resulting in a complete reorientation. Head fights with heart, the thinker becomes a feeler, the feeler a thinker.

Our own values and norms emerge. The family is left behind. Our destiny becomes visible in our contact with others. Sexuality becomes active. We begin to see people as girls and boys, men and women. We explore, discover, or retreat and lock ourselves up. Our attitudes toward our own sex and the other may be determined for life during this phase. When the wheel stops turning at the end of this phase, we feel relieved. We command a view of the world and can say, "So this is what it's all about."

## THE FOURTH PHASE
## 21 TO 28 YEARS
## ALONE AND TOGETHER

In the fourth phase, we say good-bye to our earlier peer groups. Deeper personal friendships, love relationships, and more complex social contacts come in their place. The relationship with the first group we belonged to—our family—becomes important again.

We develop further and continue to learn. We have become people; we have our own opinions and directions in life. We experiment with our talents, doing this and that, but who we really are still eludes us. We are still apprentices to life.

At the end of this period, the phase of personality development is over. We have grown up.

## THE FIFTH PHASE
## 28 TO 35 YEARS
## ENTERING THE WORLD

The fifth phase involves entering life to the full. The apprenticeship is over, and we realize that each of us has a unique task in life.

New urges or stimuli, possibly resulting in drastic changes, will have to be assimilated, especially at the beginning of this period. These impulses will have to be worked out in the world at large, in contrast to similar impulses at puberty, which were worked out in the private sphere.

In this phase we express ourselves, searching for our own styles. We wrestle free from old styles and leave them behind.

Ease of mind and certainty of direction come gradually, as does our way in society.

49

56

63

70

77

84

## THE SIXTH PHASE
## 35 TO 42 YEARS
## CRYSTALLIZATION

This phase offers us the possibility to join heart, head, *and* hands—feelings, thoughts, *and* deeds. Feeling and thinking can now be in agreement. Our deeds can now reflect how we *really* feel about things. The alternative is moral corruption.

The fullness of form is achieved. Everything learned and experienced to date crystallizes into a definite product, which is then offered with the greatest possible confidence to the community. The continuity of the community is served by our offering.

At the crossroads of continuity (which is highly valued by society) and discontinuity (which is essential for the individual), the midlife crisis develops.

## THE SEVENTH PHASE
## 42 TO 49 YEARS
## THROUGH THE
## LABYRINTH

In the seventh phase, life's autumn begins. You have passed the halfway mark, and you know it.

There's nothing you can do that you haven't already done, and everything you have done before has left its mark. You are surrounded by self-created forms and structures that have begun to lead their own lives. These creations now form a labyrinth, through which you try to find a way.

Gradually, you begin to see the relativity of things, but how to deal with unfulfillment remains a central question.

This is a period of purification. If you dare to find your way in the dark to the heart of the labyrinth and meet yourself there, including the selves that you *don't* want to be, fear falls away. You begin to realize that forms, structures, and relationships might actually be expressions of life itself.

## THE EIGHTH PHASE
## 49 TO 56 YEARS
## GUIDING AND BEING
## GUIDED

You guide and are guided. You have made it through the labyrinth, thanks to the thread of love that was continually placed in your hands. Realizing this, you are thankful and gain the right to guide others.

The power of the outer world begins to wane, the inner world emerges more and more. If you shut yourself off from this inner world, you have only two possibilities: You resist the passage of time and try desperately to hold on to youth, or you succumb to the power of time, your energies extinguished.

You take stock of your life. What have you really achieved? What can you be proud of? Were you nothing more than a replaceable cog in a giant machine?

The game of trying to outshine others is over. We won or we lost. In any case, if we are still trying to play the game, then we certainly have lost.

## THE NINTH PHASE
## 56 TO 63 YEARS
## HEAVEN AND EARTH

It is sometimes painful to see that our grip on life fails. Time runs through our fingers like water. Everything passes so quickly. Yet at the same time there is that other pulse, deep within us—the steady heartbeat.

The temptation to forcefully adapt to that ever-changing world outside of our door resurfaces. If we give in to that temptation, we will be at best a poor copy of the others, eventually finding that we have painted ourselves into a corner. But if, rather than tuning in to the outer world, we tune in to our own inner sources, we will soon discover that we actually are centerpoints. As centerpoints, we offer not so much factual knowledge as insight. We are examples, pillars of strength.

A new alchemical process begins now. It gives us the chance to transform and to channel wisely the strength that has been burning away inside us since our youth. Those who know how to use this alchemy rejuvenate themselves. They transform vitality into fortitude and endurance.

# THE TENTH PHASE
## 63 TO 70 YEARS
## TOWARD SIMPLICITY

The tenth phase marks the beginning of life's winter. The appearance of things becomes less and less important. We enjoy life as it is.

In this phase, it becomes clear how much we have *lived* in the work we did. Did we do it because we had no choice—just to earn a living—or was our work something that came from inside? If the answer is the latter, we will find that the fire of life hasn't burned us to ashes or fossilized us. Rather, it has burnished us into gold. We have tapped the inner ore.

Has a portway opened from the material to the immaterial world? Then there will be no ossification. Our experience will provide us with wise answers to everyday questions. Our greatest effectiveness will be in our simplicity.

# THE ELEVENTH PHASE
## 70 TO 77 YEARS
## THROUGH DEATH

It is an ancient image: everything that happens is enclosed by the "ouroboros"—the tail-eater, the snake that bites its own tail. It marks the boundaries of all things.

This snake is the symbol of time and the laws of time to which all things are subjected. One of the most important laws, if not *the* most important, is that everything that is created must one day be destroyed. Everything that is born also dies. In others words, living in time is dying.

In some images of the ouroboros, you can see that it doesn't exist of itself; it is "let down" out of another reality that is invisible to our eyes.

This expresses the fact that the temporal world is not the ultimate reality and that death at the end of temporal reality is not a definitive end.

Death is a watcher. Death is, according to the holy books, the last opponent. Beyond it lies another reality. We cannot express what this reality will look like in the language of space and time. But the reality beyond death *is* knowable, because death is not only our last opponent, it is also our opponent *within* life.

From moment to moment, we can let ourselves be ruled by our fear, which in the final analysis is always the fear of death. We can shy away from the so-called little deaths of every day and struggle to stay as we were, whatever the cost, to keep what we had. Doing this, we resist the impulses of life—the hand that lets down the snake—and take no more risks. The paradox is that you can only escape death in death. Fleeing what we could call living death—death that breaks into the continuity of life and so opens us up to new life—we become lifeless. We become rigid, lose our thirst for life, become fixated on everything that can go wrong. We become a living dead. There is nothing anyone can do from the outside to help such a person. Unless we—from inside—turn ourselves around and, despite our fears and worries, repent to life, we remain dead. It is this living death that Jesus referred to when he said, "Let the dead bury the dead."

In the years from 70 to 77, we are fully offered the opportunity to recognize and approach death as our lifelong companion. Where we were dead so as to avoid life, now we can let life in. This phase offers us the most essential opportunity

of a second chance. In all things, the ultimate question is put forth; the answer will be ultimately redeeming.

Inherent to this second chance is the fact that you are freed from illusion, even from the strongest of all illusions—that you can somehow survive by projecting yourself forward in time, whether through your children, your work, your creations, your influence. Free of illusions, there is nothing in the temporal world that can trap you, and death as a metaphor of finality no longer affects you. "Then you die," as the German mystic Jakob Böhme put it, "before you die." On the other hand, if death catches you while you are trying to escape, you will "decay into death."

The years 70 to 77 are years of exhaustion, resignation, or acceptance, and all points in between. We resign ourselves to defeat, or we are grateful, or we have accomplished what we set out to accomplish. Letting go, we are taken up. The end of the road is in sight. Going is peace.

## THE TWELFTH PHASE
## 77 TO 84
## ETERNAL LIFE

If there is no death at the frontier of life, then life is just what it is. The world offers no promise, poses no danger. There is no future to bring what isn't already there, no other to make things better or worse. Time has become eternity, life eternal life. There is peace.

During the first phase, the child left paradise. Now, the way back is found. Returning within to unity, the child is complete.

## BIRTHDAY CALENDAR

On each birthday, you can turn a page and read what is new—what the coming year has in store for you and those nearest and dearest to you.

When you fill in the birth dates of loved ones on the following pages, note the year of their birth next to their name. That way you will always know how old they are.

## January

1 _____ ____
2 _____ ____
3 _____ ____
4 _____ ____
5 _____ ____
6 _____ ____
7 _____ ____
8 _____ ____
9 _____ ____
10 _____ ____
11 _____ ____
12 _____ ____
13 _____ ____
14 _____ ____
15 _____ ____
16 _____ ____
17 _____ ____
18 _____ ____
19 _____ ____
20 _____ ____
21 _____ ____
22 _____ ____
23 _____ ____
24 _____ ____
25 _____ ____
26 _____ ____
27 _____ ____
28 _____ ____
29 _____ ____
30 _____ ____
31 _____ ____

## February

1 _____ ____
2 _____ ____
3 _____ ____
4 _____ ____
5 _____ ____
6 _____ ____
7 _____ ____
8 _____ ____
9 _____ ____
10 _____ ____
11 _____ ____
12 _____ ____
13 _____ ____
14 _____ ____
15 _____ ____
16 _____ ____
17 _____ ____
18 _____ ____
19 _____ ____
20 _____ ____
21 _____ ____
22 _____ ____
23 _____ ____
24 _____ ____
25 _____ ____
26 _____ ____
27 _____ ____
28 _____ ____
29 _____ ____

## March

1 _____ ___
2 _____ ___
3 _____ ___
4 _____ ___
5 _____ ___
6 _____ ___
7 _____ ___
8 _____ ___
9 _____ ___
10 _____ ___
11 _____ ___
12 _____ ___
13 _____ ___
14 _____ ___
15 _____ ___
16 _____ ___
17 _____ ___
18 _____ ___
19 _____ ___
20 _____ ___
21 _____ ___
22 _____ ___
23 _____ ___
24 _____ ___
25 _____ ___
26 _____ ___
27 _____ ___
28 _____ ___
29 _____ ___
30 _____ ___
31 _____ ___

## April

1 _____ ___
2 _____ ___
3 _____ ___
4 _____ ___
5 _____ ___
6 _____ ___
7 _____ ___
8 _____ ___
9 _____ ___
10 _____ ___
11 _____ ___
12 _____ ___
13 _____ ___
14 _____ ___
15 _____ ___
16 _____ ___
17 _____ ___
18 _____ ___
19 _____ ___
20 _____ ___
21 _____ ___
22 _____ ___
23 _____ ___
24 _____ ___
25 _____ ___
26 _____ ___
27 _____ ___
28 _____ ___
29 _____ ___
30 _____ ___

May

1 _____  ____
2 _____  ____
3 _____  ____
4 _____  ____
5 _____  ____
6 _____  ____
7 _____  ____
8 _____  ____
9 _____  ____
10 _____  ____
11 _____  ____
12 _____  ____
13 _____  ____
14 _____  ____
15 _____  ____
16 _____  ____
17 _____  ____
18 _____  ____
19 _____  ____
20 _____  ____
21 _____  ____
22 _____  ____
23 _____  ____
24 _____  ____
25 _____  ____
26 _____  ____
27 _____  ____
28 _____  ____
29 _____  ____
30 _____  ____
31 _____  ____

June

1 _____  ____
2 _____  ____
3 _____  ____
4 _____  ____
5 _____  ____
6 _____  ____
7 _____  ____
8 _____  ____
9 _____  ____
10 _____  ____
11 _____  ____
12 _____  ____
13 _____  ____
14 _____  ____
15 _____  ____
16 _____  ____
17 _____  ____
18 _____  ____
19 _____  ____
20 _____  ____
21 _____  ____
22 _____  ____
23 _____  ____
24 _____  ____
25 _____  ____
26 _____  ____
27 _____  ____
28 _____  ____
29 _____  ____
30 _____  ____

## July

1 _____ ___
2 _____ ___
3 _____ ___
4 _____ ___
5 _____ ___
6 _____ ___
7 _____ ___
8 _____ ___
9 _____ ___
10 _____ ___
11 _____ ___
12 _____ ___
13 _____ ___
14 _____ ___
15 _____ ___
16 _____ ___
17 _____ ___
18 _____ ___
19 _____ ___
20 _____ ___
21 _____ ___
22 _____ ___
23 _____ ___
24 _____ ___
25 _____ ___
26 _____ ___
27 _____ ___
28 _____ ___
29 _____ ___
30 _____ ___
31 _____ ___

## August

1 _____ ___
2 _____ ___
3 _____ ___
4 _____ ___
5 _____ ___
6 _____ ___
7 _____ ___
8 _____ ___
9 _____ ___
10 _____ ___
11 _____ ___
12 _____ ___
13 _____ ___
14 _____ ___
15 _____ ___
16 _____ ___
17 _____ ___
18 _____ ___
19 _____ ___
20 _____ ___
21 _____ ___
22 _____ ___
23 _____ ___
24 _____ ___
25 _____ ___
26 _____ ___
27 _____ ___
28 _____ ___
29 _____ ___
30 _____ ___
31 _____ ___

## September

1 _____ ____
2 _____ ____
3 _____ ____
4 _____ ____
5 _____ ____
6 _____ ____
7 _____ ____
8 _____ ____
9 _____ ____
10 _____ ____
11 _____ ____
12 _____ ____
13 _____ ____
14 _____ ____
15 _____ ____
16 _____ ____
17 _____ ____
18 _____ ____
19 _____ ____
20 _____ ____
21 _____ ____
22 _____ ____
23 _____ ____
24 _____ ____
25 _____ ____
26 _____ ____
27 _____ ____
28 _____ ____
29 _____ ____
30 _____ ____

## October

1 _____ ____
2 _____ ____
3 _____ ____
4 _____ ____
5 _____ ____
6 _____ ____
7 _____ ____
8 _____ ____
9 _____ ____
10 _____ ____
11 _____ ____
12 _____ ____
13 _____ ____
14 _____ ____
15 _____ ____
16 _____ ____
17 _____ ____
18 _____ ____
19 _____ ____
20 _____ ____
21 _____ ____
22 _____ ____
23 _____ ____
24 _____ ____
25 _____ ____
26 _____ ____
27 _____ ____
28 _____ ____
29 _____ ____
30 _____ ____
31 _____ ____

## November

1 _____ \_\_\_\_
2 _____ \_\_\_\_
3 _____ \_\_\_\_
4 _____ \_\_\_\_
5 _____ \_\_\_\_
6 _____ \_\_\_\_
7 _____ \_\_\_\_
8 _____ \_\_\_\_
9 _____ \_\_\_\_
10 _____ \_\_\_\_
11 _____ \_\_\_\_
12 _____ \_\_\_\_
13 _____ \_\_\_\_
14 _____ \_\_\_\_
15 _____ \_\_\_\_
16 _____ \_\_\_\_
17 _____ \_\_\_\_
18 _____ \_\_\_\_
19 _____ \_\_\_\_
20 _____ \_\_\_\_
21 _____ \_\_\_\_
22 _____ \_\_\_\_
23 _____ \_\_\_\_
24 _____ \_\_\_\_
25 _____ \_\_\_\_
26 _____ \_\_\_\_
27 _____ \_\_\_\_
28 _____ \_\_\_\_
29 _____ \_\_\_\_
30 _____ \_\_\_\_

## December

1 _____ \_\_\_\_
2 _____ \_\_\_\_
3 _____ \_\_\_\_
4 _____ \_\_\_\_
5 _____ \_\_\_\_
6 _____ \_\_\_\_
7 _____ \_\_\_\_
8 _____ \_\_\_\_
9 _____ \_\_\_\_
10 _____ \_\_\_\_
11 _____ \_\_\_\_
12 _____ \_\_\_\_
13 _____ \_\_\_\_
14 _____ \_\_\_\_
15 _____ \_\_\_\_
16 _____ \_\_\_\_
17 _____ \_\_\_\_
18 _____ \_\_\_\_
19 _____ \_\_\_\_
20 _____ \_\_\_\_
21 _____ \_\_\_\_
22 _____ \_\_\_\_
23 _____ \_\_\_\_
24 _____ \_\_\_\_
25 _____ \_\_\_\_
26 _____ \_\_\_\_
27 _____ \_\_\_\_
28 _____ \_\_\_\_
29 _____ \_\_\_\_
30 _____ \_\_\_\_
31 _____ \_\_\_\_

## ABOUT THE AUTHOR

Hans Korteweg is a well-respected Jungian scholar who, with his wife, Hanneke, directs the Institute for Applied Psychology, a retreat and study center located in the Netherlands. He has written five books that explore life from a philosophical perspective.

## ABOUT THE ILLUSTRATOR

Erica Duvekot is an art therapist who has also taught and has worked in art, design, and theater. She recently published a book entitled *Teachings of a Courtisane*. Because of her ability to translate his words to images, Hans Korteweg asked Erica to illustrate this book.